Jake Rowley is a barrister at Farrar's Building specialising in high value personal injury litigation. His experience spans the full spectrum of such claims including those arising from road traffic accidents; employer's liability; public liability; and occupier's liability claims. His clients include private individuals, local authorities, major UK insurance companies, well-known national and international commercial entities, and National Governments.

Jake has a particular interest in, and significant experience of, cases involving allegations of fraud and/or fundamental dishonesty. A substantial proportion of Jake's caseload involves accusations of dishonesty including, allegedly fabricated accidents; staged or induced collisions; phantom passenger/occupancy cases; low-velocity impacts; 'late presentation' claims; malingering; and fabricated or exaggerated injuries. Jake brings a meticulous and forensic approach to his consideration of the evidence and prides himself on conducting thorough and robust cross-examinations at trial. Jake is regularly invited to speak or provide training on the law and practice relating to fundamental dishonesty to both solicitors and insurers.

Fundamental Dishonesty and QOCS in Personal Injury Proceedings: Law and Practice

Fundamental Dishonesty and QOCS in Personal Injury Proceedings: Law and Practice

Jake Rowley
Barrister
Farrar's Building, Temple

Law Brief Publishing

Published 2020 by Law Brief Publishing, an imprint of Law Brief Publishing Ltd
30 The Parks
Minehead
Somerset
TA24 8BT

www.lawbriefpublishing.com

Paperback: 978-1-913715-60-1

For my Mum.

For your unwavering support, your inexhaustible encouragement, and your continual belief. For being my constant source of strength, my grounding influence, my inspiration, my closest friend, and my greatest champion. For reminding me to always 'keep the faith', and for keeping it with me.

For all that you have done, and for all that I know you will unhesitatingly always do.

The journey would not have been possible without you.

And for Luke.

Gone, but never forgotten. You are so loved and so missed.

To make you proud.

PREFACE

It is no exaggeration to say that for every practitioner involved in personal injury litigation, a comprehensive understanding of the concept of fundamental dishonesty, both as it relates to Qualified One-Way Costs Shifting ("QOCS") and as it relates to s. 57 of the Criminal Justice and Courts Act 2015, is absolutely essential. It is simply not possible to carry on practice in this area of law without an intimate working knowledge of these principles and how they apply in real terms.

The law has developed significantly since the notion of fundamental dishonesty was first thrust into the spotlight at the time of its introduction into civil litigation on the 1st April 2013 as an exception to the QOCS regime. Most importantly since that time the term has been adopted within s. 57 of the Criminal Justice and Courts Act 2015; a significant piece of legislation representing a fundamental change in the law as it stood after the Supreme Court's decision in *Summers v Fairclough Homes,* which now requires the dismissal of an otherwise compensable claim where the Claimant is found to be fundamentally dishonest.

To consider and analyse the law in this vitally important area, as well as provide insight and commentary from a practical perspective, this book specifically addresses:

- The meanings of 'dishonesty' and 'fundamental';
- The relevant Civil Procedure Rules governing QOCS and fundamental dishonesty;
- Practice points as to the Defence and conduct at trial;
- Fundamental dishonesty in credit hire cases;

- When a Court can be invited to make a finding of fundamental dishonesty;
- What happens following a Claimant's discontinuance;
- The relevant Civil Procedure Rules concerning costs assessments;
- The origins of s. 57 of the Criminal Justice and Courts Act 2015;
- The meaning of 'fundamentally dishonesty' in the context of s. 57;
- Other relevant authorities dealing with s. 57;
- The meaning of 'substantial injustice'; and
- The timing of a s. 57 application.

This book is written with both legal practitioners (Claimant and Defendant) and insurers in mind.

The law as stated in this book is considered to be correct, and accurate, as at the 28th September 2020.

Jake Rowley
September 2020

CONTENTS

CHAPTER ONE
INTRODUCTION

This book seeks to consider the law and practice relating to 'fundamental dishonesty' as it is encountered in the context of personal injury claims.

Broadly speaking, the concept of 'fundamental dishonesty' arises in two different but equally important circumstances. In brief, they can be summarised as follows:

(a) First, a Defendant's application to the Court for permission to enforce against the Claimant a costs order made in the Defendant's favour, which is otherwise unenforceable by reason of the automatic operation of the Qualified One-Way Costs Shifting regime ("QOCS"); and

(b) Secondly, a Defendant's application to dismiss, in its entirety, an otherwise meritorious claim in relation to which the Claimant is *prima facie* entitled to damages, on the basis that the Claimant has been 'fundamentally dishonest' in his/her pursuit of the claim.

As will be clear, the distinction is therefore as between, on the one hand, a question of costs; and on the other, the dismissal of a *prima facie* compensable claim on the basis that it is infected by dishonesty.

The origins of the term 'fundamental dishonesty' are to be found in the Civil Procedure Rules ("CPR") where it was first used in relation to the issue of costs. However, as will be seen, the concept and its terminology, were subsequently adopted in primary legislation, namely, section 57 of the Criminal Justice and Courts Act 2015 (hereafter "s.

57 of the 2015 Act"), which governs the second of the two identified scenarios.

This is a constantly developing area of the law in which practitioners continue to attempt to explore and define the application and limits of the principles involved.

This book will broadly divide into (i) consideration of 'fundamental dishonesty' in the context of CPR r. 44.16(1) and the issue of costs; and (ii) consideration of 'fundamental dishonesty' in the context of s. 57 of the 2015 Act.

SECTION (I)

LEGAL DEFINITIONS

CHAPTER TWO
THE MEANING OF "DISHONESTY"

To understand what is meant by 'fundamental dishonesty' one must first understand two discrete matters:

(a) First, as a matter of law, what is "dishonesty"?; and

(b) Secondly, where there is proven dishonesty, what characteristics and/or qualities must that proven dishonesty possess if it is to be considered "fundamental"; and furthermore, "fundamental" in relation to what?

The Courts have provided answers to these questions.

<u>*Ivey v Genting Casinos UK Ltd* [2017] UKSC 67</u>

In *Ivey v Genting Casinos UK Ltd* [2017] UKSC 67, the Supreme Court expounded the test which is to be applied when the Court is determining whether a Claimant has acted 'dishonestly'.

Facts

Phil Ivey is a well-known and highly successful professional gambler. Over two days in August 2012, he deployed what was described by the Court as a "*highly specialist*" technique called 'edge-sorting' when playing the card game Punto Banco Baccarat at the Defendant's casino. The game is not normally, to any extent, a game of skill; it is simply a game of luck.

Broadly speaking, 'edge-sorting' works as follows. As a result of the manufacturing process of certain patterned playing cards, whilst the backs of the cards *appear* essentially identical, there are in fact *very* slight (described by the Supreme Court in this case as "*sub-millimetric*") differences between individual cards in that the pattern on the back is not precisely symmetrical. Accordingly, the pattern on the back [in the instant case a white circle broken by two curved lines] is, to that very limited extent, closer to one long edge of the card (edge A), than it is to the other long edge (edge B). Given that, before it is dealt from a card shoe, a card sits face down at the bottom of the shoe displaying one of its two long edges, it is thus possible for a sharp-eyed person sitting close to the shoe to see which long edge (whether edge A or edge B) it is. Of course, simply knowing which edge is displayed tells a gambler nothing about the value of the next card in the shoe. In order for the technique to be useful, the cards need to be sorted in some way.

As Mr Ivey played through the shoe of cards and, under the guise of 'trying to improve his luck', he requested that the croupier rotate certain cards which had been dealt (those which were statistically more likely to result in a winning hand when the shoe was subsequently played through again) in a particular way, before they were reinserted into the shoe. Given that statistically advantageous cards had thus all been unknowingly sorted in a particular fashion by the croupier, when the shoe was subsequently replayed, Mr Ivey was able to deploy the "edge-sorting" technique to identify (as a result of the very slight differences between edge A and edge B) which of the cards that had been dealt was statistically more likely to result in a winning hand, and bet on them accordingly. That process gave him a long-term advantage over the house of approximately 6.5% if the game was played perfectly accurately.

Over the course of his playing, Mr Ivey won approximately £7.7 million.

The casino declined to pay, taking the view that what he had done amounted to cheating. At trial, Mr Ivey frankly admitted that he had engaged in 'edge-sorting', and maintained that he was not cheating but rather, deploying a perfectly legitimate advantage. He considered he had done nothing unlawful and that he was not cheating.

Decision of the Supreme Court

In determining the appeal, the Supreme Court was required to consider what test should be applied when considering whether a particular claimant had been "dishonest". Lord Hughes, at [74], said as follows:

> "*When dishonesty is in question the fact-finding tribunal must first ascertain (subjectively) the actual state of the individual's knowledge or belief as to the facts. The reasonableness or otherwise of his belief is a matter of evidence (often in practice determinative) going to whether he held the belief, but it is not an additional requirement that his belief must be reasonable; the question is whether it is genuinely held. When once his actual state of mind as to knowledge or belief as to facts is established, the question whether his conduct was honest or dishonest is to be determined by the fact-finder by applying the (objective) standards of ordinary decent people. There is no requirement that the defendant must appreciate that what he has done is, by those standards, dishonest*".

The decision in *Ivey* marked an important harmonisation of the civil and criminal law vis-à-vis the relevant test for 'dishonesty', and represented a significant departure from the previously understood position following the criminal case of *R v Ghosh* [1982] QB 1053, CA, in which a two stage test for dishonesty was expounded requiring answers to the questions: (i) whether the conduct complained of was dishonest by the lay objective standards of ordinary reasonable people; and; (ii) whether the person whose conduct was being considered must have realised that ordinary honesty people would so regard his behaviour. Only if the answer to both questions was 'yes' would a person, applying the *Ghosh* test, have previously been found to have been dishonest. *Ivey* confirms the erroneousness of that two-staged approach – there is only one, objective standard to be applied; there is no secondary 'subjective' limb to the test.

CHAPTER THREE
THE MEANING OF "FUNDAMENTAL"

The meaning of 'fundamental', in the context of 'fundamental dishonesty' has been considered in a number of cases.

Michael Joseph Gosling v (1) Hailo; (2) Screwfix Direct (Cambridge County Court) (29/4/2014) (HHJ Moloney Q.C.)

Gosling, the decision of a highly respected Circuit Judge in Cambridge, was the first reported case dealing with the correct interpretation of the relevant test which is to be applied.

Facts

The Claimant suffered a serious injury to his knee a result of an accident involving a ladder manufactured by the First Defendant and sold to him by the Second Defendant. He brought claims in negligence against both Defendants on the basis that his accident had been caused by the deficient construction of the ladder. His claim included a sum for general damages for pain, suffering, and loss of amenity, and consequential losses totalling £39,000 odd, including a claim for future care of £17,000. The Defendants carried out covert surveillance on the Claimant, including on the day on which he was due to be examined by the Defendants' expert. In his witness statement, the claimant made various assertions as to his ongoing pain and disability. The Defendants subsequently disclosed the surveillance evidence to the Claimant and his experts. Inter alia, in a joint report between the parties' experts, the doctors concluded that there was no evidence of ongoing constant knee pain, as the Claimant had reported, and that the inference to be drawn resulting from the disparity between the Claimant's examination findings and the surveillance evidence (which suggested that the

Claimant had no problem) was that the Claimant was not being honest about his symptoms and his ongoing issues.

The Claimant then served a revised Schedule of Loss which was drastically reduced in value. It totally abandoned the claim for future care. The Second Defendant indicated to the Claimant that it intended to argue that the claim was fundamentally dishonesty.

Shortly before trial, the Claimant settled his claim against the First Defendant and discontinued against the Second Defendant. By operation of CPR r. 38.6, the Second Defendant therefore automatically had a costs order arising in its favour, however subject to QOCS.

Defendant's Application and Argument

The Defendant made an application under r. 44.16(1) to permit enforcement on the basis that the claim was fundamentally dishonest. The Second Defendant argued that the claim was dishonest in relation to the issue of liability – it was said that the Claimant was lying about the circumstances of the accident because he had advanced two different accounts of how it had supposedly occurred. It was argued that the latter account on which he subsequently relied at trial was dishonestly tailored to meet notice he had received from the Second Defendant that their expert had concluded the original version of events advanced suggested that the Claimant had failed to erect the ladder correctly and had thus caused his own accident. Importantly, it was also said that there was dishonesty in relation to the quantum aspect of the claim.

Decision of the Judge

HHJ Maloney Q.C. considered that the evidence in relation to the liability argument was not so clear that it could justly be determined on the papers without hearing oral evidence and that it was not proportionate to have a substantive oral hearing, including calling the Claimant and expert witnesses who had opined on the issue. The Judge declined to direct that there be a determination of the issue of dishonesty as it arose in relation to liability.

The issue concerning the Claimant's claim for damages, and dishonesty in relation to quantum, was different. The Judge considered that the surveillance was "*devastating*". Although the Claimant had a crutch in the back of his van, he was seen driving to a warehouse superstore and then spending the best part of an hour, walking without a crutch or other support. He was seen bending to pick up goods. He pushed the shopping trolley himself. He loaded the goods into his van. He then went to Asda and had lunch with his wife, without using a crutch. Later that afternoon he attended a medico-legal appointment with the Second Defendant's expert. At the hospital he got out of the van, retrieved an elbow crutch from the back, and walked into the hospital using it. He had it with him throughout the appointment. He used it when emerging from the hospital and getting back into his car. The Claimant described his complaints to the expert as constant pain in the knee, worse when walking; the more he walked the more painful it became; the pain limited his walking distance; he walked with one crutch in his left hand; he normally went shopping with his wife, with him driving the car and waiting in the car whilst she did the shopping using either her wheelchair or crutches; the pain interfered with all of his daily activities. The Judge noted that such statements had been made to the doctor within 3 hours of the Claimant having spent 45 minutes walking around a shop with his wife, himself collecting goods, and pushing the trolley and taking it to the car. As a result of the Claimant's presentation (and before seeing the surveillance), the Second Defendant's expert had concluded that the Claimant suffered with constant pain meaning it was probably appropriate for him to receive outside help for between 1 – 2 hours/week.

It was argued on his behalf that the Claimant's conduct, even if as a result of some degree of culpable exaggeration, did not make the claim 'fundamentally dishonest' as a matter of law.

HHJ Maloney Q.C. considered the meaning of "fundamental" in the context of the QOCS provisions and held as follows:

> 43. *"[...] Neither party took me to any authority on the term in question. Of course, the term "fundamental" is used in various legal contexts that are of little assistance to us here. Dictionary definitions were produced and relied upon; for example, that which was fundamental was "of, or pertaining to, the basis or groundwork of something", "going to the root of the matter", "serving as the base or foundation", "essential or indispensable".*
>
> 44. *It appears to me that this phrase in the rules has to be interpreted purposively and contextually in the light of the context. This is, of course, the determination of whether the claimant is "deserving", as Jackson LJ put it, of the protection (from the costs liability that would otherwise fall on him) extended, for reasons of social policy, by the QOCS rules. It appears to me that when one looks at the matter in that way, one sees that what the rules are doing is distinguishing between two levels of dishonesty: dishonesty in relation to the claim which is not fundamental so as to expose such a claimant to costs liability, and dishonesty which is fundamental, so as to give rise to costs liability.*
>
> 45. *The corollary term to "fundamental" would be a word with some such meaning as "incidental" or "collateral". Thus, a claimant should not be exposed to costs liability merely because he is shown to have been dishonest as to some collateral matter or perhaps as to some minor, self-contained head of damage. If, on the other hand, the dishonesty went to the root of either the whole of his claim or a substantial part of his claim, then it appears to me that it would be a fundamentally dishonest claim: a claim which depended as to a substantial or important part of itself upon dishonesty."*

The Judge felt that it was a useful exercise to look at the value of each head of loss in the context of the claim as a whole. The overall valuation (including CRU reimbursements) was approximately £80,000 before the Claimant received the surveillance evidence, including general damages of approximately £40,000 i.e. the case was approximately 50% general damages and 50% special damages. A substantial element of the special damages (£17,000) related to future care, which was substantially dependent on the Claimant's evidence in relation to his pain and discomfort. The Judge considered what the likely award for general damages would have been in relation to the injury *actually sustained*, disregarding the Claimant's assertions of significant ongoing pain. On a reasonably rough and ready basis, the Judge considered around half of the claim for general damages (i.e. approximately £20,000) would be attributable to serious ongoing pain and lack of function in the knee. On the basis that the future care claim, and a large proportion of general damages (i.e. approximately £37,000 in total) was dishonest, and that such dishonesty represented such a large part of the claim (a little over 46%) it was sufficient for the entire claim to be considered 'fundamentally dishonest'.

HHJ Maloney Q.C. observed that, as a matter of law, it was not necessary that:

> *50. "... the dishonesty went to the root either of liability as a whole, or damages in their entirety. It must be the case that dishonesty fundamental to a sufficiently major part of the claim would suffice to deprive the claimant of his costs protection, and open him to the court's discretion as to how much of the costs he should pay..."*

The Judge considered that the Claimant's dishonesty was sufficient both in relation to its "*size and importance*" [at 58] in the context of his claim for damages as a whole

Leonel Zimi v London Central Bus Company Limited (Central London County Court) (8/1/2015) (HHJ Madge)

Zimi concerned a road traffic accident. The Claimant alleged that he was stationary in the right hand lane when the driver of the Defendant's bus, moved from the left hand lane, encroaching into the Claimant's lane and in doing so, collided with the rear passenger side of his stationary vehicle, causing the Claimant to sustain personal injury and consequential loss totalling £127. The Defendant denied that there had been a collision at all between the vehicles and relied on CCTV footage tending to suggest that was correct.

HHJ Madge was not satisfied there had been a collision at all but, even if there had been one, held that the Defendant's bus had been stationary at the material time and thus, any collision was as a result of the Claimant's own negligent driving.

The Judge's attention was drawn to the decision in *Gosling*. He remarked when considering the meaning of "fundamental" [at 28], *"I assume that the word, fundamental, means something going to the base, something going to the core of the claim, something of central importance and something which is crucial."*

HHJ Madge considered that this was not a claim which could have been brought by the Claimant with a mistaken belief. The Claimant could not have had an honest belief that there was a collision of the kind claimed. This was not a case of the Claimant being naïve or unworldly. The Judge was satisfied that the Claimant's claim was 'fundamentally dishonest'. The Judge then went on to consider the exercise of his discretion under r. 44.16 and whether it was just to exercise it so as to apply the exception to QOCS. He considered it was just to do so, having regard to all the circumstances.

Brian Creech v (1) Apple Security Group Limited; (2) Severn Valley Railway (Holdings) Plc; (2) Irvin Leisure Entertainments Limited (Telford C.C., 25/3/15) (DJ Rogers)

The Claimant claimed to have been injured when on patrol as a security guard at the Severn Valley Railway Station in Kidderminster. He asserted that he had fallen over a pile of abandoned mats which had been part of a temporary ice rink that had been erected and put on the station during the school half term some weeks before. He claimed the mats had been inappropriately left, placed between three benches in the middle of the station concourse. As a result of his fall he sustained a fracture of the humerus. At trial, the Claimant did not pursue the claim against his employer, the First Defendant. The Second Defendant was the entity responsible for the station and the Third Defendant had arranged for the provision of the temporary ice rink through sub-contractors. Following trial, the claim against the Third Defendant was all but abounded on the basis it was no longer sustainable.

Both the Second and Third Defendants denied that the accident could have happened as the Claimant alleged for the simple reason that the temporary ice rink was not removed until after the Claimant purported to have sustained his fall.

DJ Rogers preferred the Defendants' evidence and concluded that the Claimant had not established that he fell over a pile of mats left on the station concourse. The Judge accepted that the rink had not been removed until after the time of the Claimant's alleged fall. The Judge considered this was not a case where there was room for error – either the Claimant was correct in his recollection and assertion that the ice rink had been removed, and partially sorted at the side of the concourse leaving piles of matting on which he fell, or he was wrong. The Second Defendant invited the Court to make a finding that the claim was '*fundamentally dishonest*'.

DJ Rogers referred to the decision in *Gosling*. The Judge conclude that the case was 'fundamentally dishonest' – the accident could not have occurred, and did not occur, in anything like the circumstances suggested by the Claimant. Although the Judge expressly shied away from using the word 'dishonesty'[1] he concluded that the case advanced by the Claimant must have been, to his knowledge, incorrect. He must have known the accident did not occur as he alleged. The Judge held that the "*... advancing of a case so plainly against the weight of the evidence, in the circumstances that I have outlined, can only be described as a fundamentally dishonest claim...*".

(1) Lorna Howlett; (2) Justin Howlett v (1) Penelope Davis; (2) Ageas Insurance Limited [2017] EWCA Civ 1696

The meaning of the word 'fundamental' was finally authoritatively confirmed by the Court of Appeal in *Howlett* which is now **the** authority on the point.

Facts and First Instance Decision

The Claimants brought proceedings in relation to personal injury and other losses said to arise from a road traffic accident on the 27th March 2013. They claimed to be passengers in a car driven by the First Defendant when it hit a parked vehicle and that the collision was caused by the First Defendant's negligence. The Second Defendant was the First Defendant's insurer who robustly defended the claim, indicating in its Defence that it did not accept the accident occurred as alleged, or at all, and requiring the Claimants to prove: that they were involved in the accident; that it was caused by the First Defendant's negligence; and that they suffered injury.

The Defence specifically pleaded that the collision was a low velocity impact, with injury being unforeseeable in any event. The Claimants'

1 The Judge's decision to expressly avoid using the language of 'dishonesty' is not readily explicable.

credibility was expressly stated to be in issue and the Second Defendant asserted that the Claimants would be required to prove their case against the backdrop of a series of facts, or contentions. which were fully set out in the Defence. These included:

- Matters which the Second Defendant suggested showed that the Claimants had been involved in previous staged/contrived accidents;
- The failure by the Second Claimant to disclose an earlier accident to his expert;
- The high number of previous road traffic accidents that the First Defendant had been involved in in the recent past;
- The fact the First Defendant had not co-operated with her insurer; and
- The unlikely/uncorroborated journey purpose.

The Second Defendant did not assert a positive case of fraud in its Defence.

At trial, the Second Defendant argued that neither of the Claimants were in the First Defendants car when the alleged accident occurred, that their claims were simply opportunistic and, further, if they were in the car, they had not suffered injury as alleged.

The trial judge, DDJ Taylor, dismissed the claim. He wholly rejected the Claimants case, essentially on the basis that none of the evidence was reliable. He considered that he had been given so many contrasting stories about the circumstances surrounding the accident; what led up to the accident; the accident itself; what happened post-accident; what evidence was given (or not given) to the medical experts; and misleading accounts set out in documents before the Court that there was,

"*...not one part of the stories explained to me by Mr and Mrs Howlett that gives me any confidence that the accident as described by them and Ms Davies on 27 March 2013 happened as described or at all*". The Judge found that the Claimants had not sustained any injury.

DDJ Taylor considered that it was open to him to find that the Claimants had been dishonest. He considered that the issue of the Claimants' honesty had been fairly identified in the Defence, and their honesty had been appropriately challenged in cross-examination with Counsel putting the Second Defendant's case to them and with the Claimants being given an opportunity to answer those allegations. The Judge found that it was "*perfectly clear*" the claim was fundamentally dishonesty.

The Claimants appealed the finding of fundamental dishonesty. That appeal was dismissed by HHJ Blair Q.C. A second appeal to the Court of Appeal followed.

Decision of the Court of Appeal

At paragraph 16, the Court of Appeal endorsed as being "*common sense*" the approach adopted by HHJ Moloney Q.C. in *Gosling* at paragraphs 44 and 45 of that judgment [as set out above, earlier in this chapter].

CHAPTER FOUR
A SUMMARY OF THE POSITION

Having received the Court of Appeal's endorsement in *Howlett*, the interpretation given to the word 'fundamental' by HHJ Maloney Q.C., as set out at paragraphs 44 and 45 of the decision in *Gosling,* now represents the authoritative statement of the law.

'Fundamental dishonesty' is dishonesty which goes to the root of either the whole claim or a substantial part of it; a 'fundamentally dishonesty' claim is one which depends to a substantial or important part of itself upon dishonesty. Dishonesty will not be 'fundamental' if it goes to some collateral matter or to some minor, self-contained head of damage.

Where dishonesty is alleged in relation to quantum, an assessment of the value of the dishonest element(s) of the claim, expressed as a percentage of the whole claim actually advanced, can be a useful tool (as in *Gosling* itself).

Moreover, it will always be important to bear in mind, that the Court's consideration of these issues is underpinned with a determination of whether, as a matter of social policy, the Claimant remains "deserving" of ongoing QOCS protection.

SECTION (II)

CPR R. 44.16(1) – THE COSTS ISSUE

CHAPTER FIVE
THE RELEVANT CIVIL PROCEDURE RULES

To obtain a proper understanding of 'fundamental dishonesty' vis-à-vis the enforcement of a costs order, it is first necessary to understand its position within the context of the QOCS regime, to which it provides an exception.

The relevant Civil Procedure Rules in relation to QOCS are contained in Section II of Part 44. CPR r. 44.13 sets out those proceedings to which QOCS applies:

"Qualified one-way costs shifting: scope and interpretation

44.13

(1) This Section applies to proceedings which include a claim for damages –

(a) for personal injuries;

(b) under the Fatal Accidents Act 1976[7]*; or*

(c) which arises out of death or personal injury and survives for the benefit of an estate by virtue of section 1(1) of the Law Reform (Miscellaneous Provisions) Act 1934[8]*,*

but does not apply to applications pursuant to section 33 of the Senior Courts Act 1981[9] *or section 52 of the County Courts Act 1984*[10] *(applications for pre-action disclosure), or where rule 44.17 applies.*

(2) In this Section, 'claimant' means a person bringing a claim to which this Section applies or an estate on behalf of which such a

> *claim is brought, and includes a person making a counterclaim or an additional claim."*

A "claim for personal injuries" (as referred to in r. 44.13(1)(a)) is defined by CPR r. 2.3 as:

> *"'claim for personal injuries' means proceedings in which there is a claim for damages in respect of personal injuries to the claimant or any other person or in respect of a person's death, and 'personal injuries' includes any disease and any impairment of a person's physical or mental condition."*

CPR r. 44.14(1) enshrines the core principle of the QOCS regime:

> *"Effect of qualified one-way costs shifting*
>
> *44.14*
>
> *(1) Subject to rules 44.15 and 44.16, orders for costs made against a claimant may be enforced without the permission of the court but only to the extent that the aggregate amount in money terms of such orders does not exceed the aggregate amount in money terms of any orders for damages and interest made in favour of the claimant."*

Express exceptions to that wide-ranging principle are contained in CPR r. 44.15 and r. 44.16. For present purposes, we are concerned only with r. 44.16(1), which provides:

> *"Exceptions to qualified one-way costs shifting where permission required*
>
> *44.16*
>
> *(1) Orders for costs made against the claimant may be enforced to the full extent of such orders with the permission of the court where the*

claim is found on the balance of probabilities to be fundamentally dishonest."

It is to be noted that the relevant burden of proof is the normal civil standard – that of the 'balance of probabilities'.

The relevant procedural rules are supplemented, in the usual way, by a Practice Direction which, for present purposes, provides as follows at paragraph 12.4:

"PD 12.4

In a case to which rule 44.16(1) applies (fundamentally dishonest claims) –

(a) the court will normally direct that issues arising out of an allegation that the claim is fundamentally dishonest be determined at the trial;

(b) where the proceedings have been settled, the court will not, save in exceptional circumstances, order that issues arising out of an allegation that the claim was fundamentally dishonest be determined in those proceedings;

(c) where the claimant has served a notice of discontinuance, the court may direct that issues arising out of an allegation that the claim was fundamentally dishonest be determined notwithstanding that the notice has not been set aside pursuant to rule 38.4;

(d) the court may, as it thinks fair and just, determine the costs attributable to the claim having been found to be fundamentally dishonest."

CHAPTER SIX
PRACTICE POINTS – PLEADINGS AND CONDUCT AT TRIAL

Does 'Fundamental Dishonesty' need to be Pleaded by the Defendant?

The short answer is, 'no', 'fundamental dishonesty' does not need to be expressly pleaded in the Defence.

In *Howlett,* the Court of Appeal confirmed (at [30]) that the statement in PD 44, para 12.4, namely that the Court "*will normally direct that issues arising out of an allegation that the claim is fundamentally dishonest be determined at trial*" did not mean that for QOCS to be displaced on account of 'fundamental dishonesty', there need have been a pleading to that effect in the Defence. The Court of Appeal observed that the point of the provision in the Practice Direction was to indicate that such issues should generally be decided at the trial rather than some other stage; it did not impose any pleading requirement. The Court went on to say (at [31] – [32]):

> *"31. Statements of case are, of course, crucial to the identification of the issues between the parties and what falls to be decided by the Court. However, the mere fact that the opposing party has not alleged dishonesty in his pleadings will not necessarily bar a judge from finding a witness to have been lying: in fact, judges must regularly characterise witnesses as having been deliberately untruthful even where there has been no plea of fraud. On top of that, it seems to me that where an insurer in a case such as the present one, following the guidance given in Kearsley v Klarfeld, has denied a claim without putting forward a substantive case of fraud but setting out "the facts from which they would be inviting the judge to draw the inference that the plaintiff had not in fact suffered the injuries he asserted", it must be open to the trial judge, assuming that the relevant points*

> *have been adequately explored during the oral evidence, to state in his judgment not just that the claimant has not proved his case but that, having regard to matters pleaded in the defence, he has concluded (say) that the alleged accident did not happen or that the claimant was not present. The key question in such a case would be whether the claimant had been given adequate warning of, and a proper opportunity to deal with, the possibility of such a conclusion and the matters leading the judge to it rather than whether the insurer had positively alleged fraud in its defence.*
>
> *32. Further, I do not think an insurer need necessarily have alleged in its defence that the claim was "fundamentally dishonest" for one-way costs shifting to be displaced on that ground. Where findings properly made in the trial judge's judgment on the substantive claim warrant the conclusion that it was "fundamentally dishonest", an insurer can, I think, invoke CPR 44.16(1) regardless of whether there was any reference to fundamental dishonesty in its pleadings. To my mind, there is force in Judge Blair QC's comment (in paragraph 54 of his judgment):*
>
>> *"I observe that one does not have to plead a claim for an award of costs on the indemnity basis (as opposed to the standard basis), so why would one have to expressly plead this more remote stage of the costs determination exercise, namely for an order for the enforcement of an adverse costs order?""*

In *Howlett*, it was considered that the Second Defendant's Defence gave the Claimants sufficient notice of the points that the Second Defendant intended to raise at trial and the possibility that the Judge would reach the conclusion that the Claimants were dishonest. The Claimants could not complain of ambush. On the basis of the content of the Defence, it had been open to the trial Judge to find dishonesty, provided that matters had been properly put in cross-examination.

That being said, there is also nothing which precludes a Defendant from pleading in its Defence that it intends to invite the Court to make a finding that the Claimant has been '*fundamentally dishonest*'. In many instances, it will be advisable to do so. Such a pleading enables the Defendant to argue that the issue had been appropriately raised in early course and was 'live'; that the Claimant had been given notice of the Defendant's intentions; and the Claimant could not complain of ambush. The practice adopted in *Howlett,* namely pleading those matters forming the background against which the Claimant(s) would be required to prove his/her/their case(s) represents a sensible course which should be followed.

Moreover, whilst those settling the Defence should naturally exercise their own professional judgment on whether to include such an averment (as well as ensuring that the content of the Defence complies with the relevant requirements of Part 16 and the attendant Practice Direction) it is right to note that *strictly speaking* the stringent ethical constraints imposed on practitioners in relation to pleading a substantive allegation of fraud do not apply in relation to pleadings of '*fundamental dishonesty*'. Naturally it would, however, be entirely improper to plead an allegation which was wholly unsustainable.

How Should Matters be Approached in Cross-Examination?

In *Howlett,* Counsel for the Claimant had argued that the Claimants were not cross-examined at the trial on the basis that their claim was dishonest or even that there were dishonest aspects to it and, accordingly, it was not open for the Deputy District Judge to make any finding of dishonesty. The Second Defendant argued that it had been patently clear in cross-examination that their honesty, and not just their credibility, was being challenged.

The Court of Appeal accepted that the honesty of the Claimants' evidence was adequately explored in cross-examination. In considering the Claimant's submission, the Court of Appeal referred to prior authority and, at paragraphs [27] – [29], said:

> *27. Vogon International Ltd v Serious Fraud Office, a decision of the Court of Appeal, provides an illustration of the principle that (to quote from paragraph 29 of May LJ's judgment):*
>
> > *"It is ... elementary common fairness that neither parties to litigation, their counsel, nor judges should make serious imputations or findings in any litigation when the person against whom such imputations or findings are made have not been given a proper opportunity of dealing with the imputations and defending themselves."*
>
> (a) *In Abbey Forwarding Ltd v Hone [2010] EWHC 2029 (Ch), where the claimant alleged that certain defendants had been dishonestly complicit in excise diversion frauds, Lewison J (as he then was) noted that "before a finding of dishonesty can be made it must not only be pleaded, but also put in cross-examination" (paragraph 47) and, as regards one of these defendants, that "it was not put to [him] that he knew or suspected that the underlying transactions were fraudulent; with the result that a finding to that effect is not open to me" (paragraph 185). The Court was not, therefore, addressing the question of what a defence must contain.*
>
> (b) *In Haringey LBC v Hines, the particulars of claim alleged deceit, but the deceit case was not put to Ms Hines when she gave evidence: counsel "never grasped the critical nettle when cross-examining Ms Hines and the judge failed to grasp it when making his judgment" (to quote from Rimer LJ, at paragraph 41). The case turned, not on the pleadings, but on the "basic principle of fairness that if a party is being accused of fraud, and is then called as a witness, the particular fraud alleged should be put specifically to that party so that he/she may answer it" (paragraph 39)."*

In considering further authority on the issue the Court observed, at [34 – 35]:

> 34. *"The passages I have cited from the Abbey Forwarding and Haringey cases include references to the need to put an allegation of dishonesty to a witness. These reflect the somewhat obscurely reported decision of the House of Lords in Browne v Dunn (1894) 6 R 67. As was noted in Markem Corp v Zipher Ltd [2005] EWCA Civ 267, [2005] RPC 31 (at paragraph 58), Browne v Dunn has been cited for this proposition:*
>
> > *"Where the court is to be asked to disbelieve a witness, the witness should be cross-examined; and failure to cross-examine a witness on some material part of his evidence or at all, may be treated as an acceptance of the truth of that part or the whole of his evidence."*
>
> 35. *In Markem Corp v Zipher Ltd, the Court of Appeal cited from Browne v Dunn via an Australian decision, Allied Pastoral Holdings v Federal Commissioner of Taxation (1983) 44 ALR 607. In that latter case, Hunt J said this about, for example, Lord Herschell LC's speech in Browne v Dunn:*
>
> > *"Lord Herschell LC said (at 70–71): 'Now my Lords, I cannot help saying that it seems to me to be absolutely essential to the proper conduct of a case, where it is intended to suggest that a witness is not speaking the truth on a particular point, to direct his attention to the fact by some questions put in cross- examination showing that that imputation is intended to be made, and not to take his evidence and pass it by as a matter altogether unchallenged, and then, when it is impossible for him to explain, as perhaps he might have been able to do if such questions had been put to him, the circumstances which it is suggested indicate that the story he tells ought not to be believed, to argue that he is a witness unworthy of credit. My Lords, I*

> *have always understood that if you intended to impeach a witness you are bound, whilst he is in the box, to give him an opportunity of making any explanation which is open to him; and, as it seems to me, that is not only a rule of professional practice in the conduct of a case, but is essential to fair play and fair dealing with witnesses.*
>
> *His Lordship conceded that there was no obligation to raise such a matter in cross-examination in circumstances where it is 'perfectly clear that (the witness) has had full notice beforehand that there is an intention to impeach the credibility of the story which he is telling'. His speech continued (at 72): 'All I am saying is that it will not do to impeach the credibility of a witness upon a matter on which he has not had any opportunity of giving an explanation by reason of there having been no suggestion whatever in the course of the case that his story is not accepted.'"""*

The Court gave some useful guidance as to how allegations of dishonesty should be approached by Defendants at trial, which should clearly be followed. The Court said, at [39]:

> *"39. It is perhaps worth adding two comments. First, where a witness' honesty is to be challenged, it will always be best if that is explicitly put to the witness. There can then be no doubt that honesty is in issue. But what ultimately matters is that the witness has had fair notice of a challenge to his or her honesty and an opportunity to deal with it. It may be that in a particular context a cross-examination which does not use the words "dishonest" or "lying" will give a witness fair warning. That will be a matter for the trial judge to decide. Secondly, the fact that a party has not alleged fraud in his pleading may not preclude him from suggesting to a witness in cross-examination that he is lying. That must, in fact, be a common occurrence."*

CHAPTER SEVEN
FUNDAMENTAL DISHONESTY IN THE CONTEXT OF CREDIT HIRE

There is authority dealing with the issue of 'fundamental dishonesty' in the context of credit hire claims, which warrants consideration.

Mansur Haider v DSM Demolition Ltd [2019] EWHC 2712 (QB)

Facts and First Instance Decision

Haider concerned a claim for damages arising out of road traffic accident in July 2014. Inter alia, the Claimant brought claims for credit hire and associated losses which exceeded £30,000. In support of his claim for hire charges, the Claimant asserted that he was impecunious.

The Defendant alleged that the collision was deliberately staged and that the Claimant, in conjunction with the car in front of him, intentionally brought about the crash by braking suddenly and unnecessarily so as to cause the Defendant's insured to hit the Claimant from behind. At first instance, HHJ Tindal found that the Claimant had reasonably braked in light of the car in front of him performing a dangerous manoeuvre by turning left at the last minute, but that the Claimant "*over-braked and overreacted and came to a stop*", thereby depriving the Defendant's insured of the opportunity to stop himself. The Judge found that there was no negligence on the part of the Defendant's insured, and therefore the claim failed.

During the course of the litigation, the Claimant had signed a disclosure statement, verified by a Statement of Truth, which did not disclose that he held any credit cards. He had also been asked a series of Part 18 Questions in which he was specifically requested to list all his credit cards and supply supporting information such as credit limits and statements. In response to that question, the Claimant had replied, "*I did not have any credit card accounts*". At trial, in oral evidence, the Claimant admitted to possessing two credit cards at the relevant time. Moreover, the Claimant had been asked Part 18 Questions about his bank statements and, in his Replies to those questions, disclosed that he held one bank account with HSBC. It was put to him in cross-examination that the bank accounts disclosed did not show the paying in, by him, of a cheque in the sum of £3,800 made to him by the Defendant's insurer by way of an interim payment. In evidence, the Claimant accepted that he had another account, but stated that he had only opened one account and the bank had made an error and opened a second account in his name.

The Defendant argued before the Judge that the Claimant had not been honest in relation to both his disclosure and his evidence. HHJ Tindal took the view that there had not been 'particularly good disclosure' but that none of it had given him the impression that the Claimant had been dishonest. The Judge took the view that the inconsistencies were explicable on the basis the Claimant was trying to recall events four years ago and he was 'basically an honest man'.

Arguments on Appeal

Both parties appealed. The Claimant's appeal (as to the Judge's findings on liability) are not relevant for present purposes.

The Defendant argued that the Claimant's case was 'fundamentally dishonest' and that HHJ Tindal should have so found given, inter alia, first, the Claimant did not disclose, either on his list of documents, or in his response to Part 18 Questions, that he held two credit cards. It was said by the Defendant that the disclosure list, which was supported by a Statement of Truth, was false; the non-disclosure was a lie; and the Claimant compounded that lie in his Responses to the Part 18 Questions. Secondly, the Claimant did not disclose that he held a second bank account, but had only admitted this in cross-examination and had then claimed that the second account was opened by the bank in error.

Decision of the High Court

Julian Knowles J allowed the Defendant's appeal, finding that the claim was 'fundamentally dishonest'. His Lordship stated, at [57 – 58]:

> "*57. In my judgment* [HHJ Tindal's conclusion that there had not been 'particularly good disclosure; and that the Claimant's inconsistencies were explicable on the basis he was trying to recall events four years ago and that he was basically an honest man] *was not reasonably open to the judge. It was plainly dishonest for the Claimant not to have disclosed his credit cards or his second bank account and the accompanying documentation. The questions he was asked were not difficult (and he did not say that he had not properly understood them); they were in writing; he had time to consider his documentation; and he had the opportunity to take legal advice if he was unsure about how to answer and what to disclose. Even if he was telling the truth about his Barclaycard account having been closed, that did not relieve him of the obligation to disclose it and the associated paperwork. He gave no explanation at all for not disclosing his Vanquis Bank card, and his claim that somehow the bank had given him another account in error, into which he had just happened to pay his interim payment, was not credible. The Claimant's actual state of knowledge was that he knew full well that he had two bank account and two credit cards, and that he had concealed this information. Nor, for the reasons I have given, could the Claimant's failure be explained on the grounds that he was being asked to recall events from four years previously."*
>
> *58. I have set out the judge's reasoning but, with respect to him, he did not properly address the evidence. This was not simply a case where there had just been 'not particularly good' disclosure by the Claimant. He deliberately failed to disclose highly material evidence.*

> *There was simply no basis on which the judge could properly have concluded that the Claimant had simply got confused on these issues. The only possible reasonable inference from the evidence was that the Claimant intentionally failed to make full disclosure, and that failure can only be labelled as dishonest."*

As to the question of whether the dishonesty was 'fundamental', his Lordship considered it was: it did not relate to some collateral matter, but went to the root of a substantial part of the claim (in excess of £30,000) (at [59]).

In a warning to Claimant's in credit hire cases, his Lordship importantly stated, "*[T]he importance of the Claimant giving proper disclosure about his financial circumstances needs to be emphasised*", and he aligned himself with a submission made by Counsel for the Defendant, that "*…the County Court cannot carry out an assessment of the issue of impecuniosity when a litigant fails to give full financial disclosure. By doing as he did, the Claimant prevented the Defendant from carrying out a proper investigation into his claimed impecuniosity. This skewed and distorted the presentation of his claim in a way that can only be termed fundamentally dishonest*" (at [59]).

SECTION (III)

SEEKING A FINDING PURSUANT TO CPR R. 44.16

CHAPTER EIGHT
INTRODUCTION

As identified in Practice Direction 44, paragraph 12.4 (set out above in Chapter 5) there are three key scenarios in which the Court may be asked to deal with a request/application by a Defendant for a finding of 'fundamental dishonesty' in the context of r. 44.16(1).

The first and most obvious (and almost certainly the overwhelmingly most common) will be by way of an oral application/submission at the conclusion of a trial in which the Claimant has (per *Howlett*) been appropriately challenged in cross-examination. Such an approach is specifically identified in the Practice Direction as being the "*normal*" approach where, at paragraph 12.4(a) it confirms:

> *"(a) The court will normally direct that issues arising out of an allegation that the claim is fundamentally dishonest be determined at the trial;"*

The reasons for this are clear and obvious: the Judge will have just heard all the evidence in the trial and he/she will have had an opportunity to assess the Claimant giving evidence, their credibility. Any such Judge is therefore best placed to determine whether the Claimant has been dishonest, and whether that dishonesty was fundamental when viewed in the context of the claim as a whole. Moreover, in accordance with the Overriding Objective the Court is required to deal with cases efficiently and at proportionate cost, meaning that it should dispose of as many issues on the same occasion as possible.

The second situation arises in circumstances where, after proceedings have been settled, the Court may be invited to consider an allegation that the claim was 'fundamentally dishonest'. The availability of such an approach is specifically identified in paragraph 12.4(b) of the Practice Direction, which makes clear that the starting position is that the Court "*will not*" order that the issues arising out of such an allegation be determined, save where there are "*exceptional circumstances*". The *de facto* position is therefore that settlement will preclude consideration of allegations of 'fundamental dishonesty'. The burden of satisfying the Court that there are "*exceptional circumstances*" would clearly be on the Defendant. There is, to the writer's knowledge, no reported case dealing with the approach envisaged by PD44, paragraph 12.4(b). That is not considered surprising. It is almost inconceivable (not least in light of the implementation of s. 57 of the 2015 Act) that a Defendant would agree to the settlement of a claim, with a pre-meditated intention to attempt *thereafter* to convince a Judge to determine issues of dishonesty. Moreover, the prospect of the process envisaged by PD44, paragraph 12.4(b) being successfully invoked, in the absence of other circumstances which would otherwise invalidate the compromise in any event (e.g. subsequently uncovered fraud), must surely be vanishingly small.

The third, and more complicated scenario in which the Court may be asked to consider allegations of 'fundamental dishonesty' is following the Claimant filing a Notice of Discontinuance. This is a common occurrence with which all Defendant practitioners are likely to have some experience and it warrants closer consideration.

CHAPTER NINE
APPROACH FOLLOWING CLAIMANT'S FILING OF A NOTICE OF DISCONTINUANCE

In accordance with CPR r. 38.2(1) a Claimant may discontinue all or part of his/her claim at any time [subject to a number of express restrictions in r. 38.2(2)]. Provided a Claimant complies with the formal requirements in Part 38, for example in relation to filing and serving the relevant Notice, the claim is then at an end.

Upon discontinuance, CPR r. 38.6(1) provides a deeming provision in relation to costs:

> *"Liability for costs*
>
> *38.6*
>
> *(1) Unless the court orders otherwise, a claimant who discontinues is liable for the costs which a defendant against whom the claimant discontinues incurred on or before the date on which notice of discontinuance was served on the defendant."*

Thus, in the overwhelming majority of cases, by automatic operation of the Rules, the Defendant obtains a costs order in its favour from commencement of the proceedings up to the date of service of the Notice of Discontinuance. In a personal injury claim however, this costs order is a pyrrhic victory given the Defendant cannot (without more) actually enforce those costs against the Claimant, by reason of the QOCS provisions.

Where the Defendant forms the view (whether pre- or post- discontinuance) that there are reasonable prospects of obtaining a finding of 'fundamental dishonesty', at first blush, it might be thought with the claim having been discontinued, that the Defendant is precluded from pursing the relevant finding. That is not the case. The Practice Direction makes clear, at paragraph 12.4(c), that the Defendant may seek to persuade the Court to direct that issues arising out of an allegation that the claim was 'fundamentally dishonest' be determined, whether or not the Notice of Discontinuance has been formally set aside. Setting aside the Notice is not a necessary pre-requisite before the Court is able to make the relevant finding.

How will the Court Approach the Issue, where the Notice of Discontinuance has not been Set Aside?

First, it is clear from the use of the words, "*...the court may direct...*" that the Court has a discretion as to whether it will order that the issues be determined, at all. Secondly, if the Court decides that it *will* permit the Defendant to pursue the allegation, the form/method of the investigation/determination is also a matter for the Court's discretion.

The manner in which both limbs of the Courts discretion should be exercised has received judicial consideration on a number of occasions.

Michael Joseph Gosling v (1) Hailo; (2) Screwfix Direct

In *Gosling*, the Claimant discontinued against the Second Defendant no more than 10 days before the trial. HHJ Maloney Q.C. was required to consider whether he should make a finding of 'fundamental dishonesty' notwithstanding the Claimant's Notice of Discontinuance had not been set aside. He noted that given, at the time, these provisions were "new law" there were no known cases on the point. He stated (emphasis added):

> *"21. The best guidance that I have found as to the approach that might be adopted is in the third lecture in the implementation program, Jackson LJ's paper on technical aspects of implementation*

dated 31st October 2011, which formed an important part of the training that the judiciary received prior to the new costs regime coming into effect. In relation to that, I note in particular the emphasis that Jackson LJ places on proportionality. At para.2.3 he refers to the topic of satellite litigation and says this:

> *"Any major civil justice reform is followed by litigation in which parties test the boundaries of the new rule. A few robust Court of Appeal decisions are needed to deal with the points raised. If the rule is supplemented by an elaborate practice direction, opportunities for satellite litigation will increase exponentially, as practitioners explore the relationship between the provisions, possible interstices in the language, and so forth. One lesson from the costs war is that lawyers leave no stone unturned when it comes to arguing about costs."*

22. In s.4 of the lecture he deals with QOCS itself, and in particular at 4.3 with the zone of QOCS with which we are presently concerned, where he says this:

> *"What conduct will deprive the claimant of costs protection? This issue is discussed in the workshop materials. I agree that if the claimant's claim is fraudulent or is struck out as an abuse of process, the claimant should forfeit costs protection. However, I do not believe that either litigants or the court will be assisted by a practice direction which gives guidance on borderline cases. Any such guidance is likely to generate increased satellite litigation for the reasons set out in para.2.3 above. There is a whole Costs Bar out there just waiting to sink its teeth into the new provisions."*

[...]

24. In considering that suggestion, I bear in mind the clear guidance of Jackson LJ as to ***the manner in which these rules should be approached. I take it to be one of proportionality, efficiency and***

the avoidance, where possible, of unduly elaborate satellite litigation, by the adoption on the court's part of a just, but wherever possible efficient and summary approach to the questions that the court is required to decide. *That would be appropriate in relation to any kind of litigation, subject to the overriding objective, but it is perhaps of particular importance when considering costs litigation itself.*

25. With that background, I turn to the questions that confront me, arising out of the rules which I have just quoted, which are brief and to the point. The first question, arising under practice direction 44 12.4(c), is this: should I direct that the issues arising out of the allegation of the claimant's fundamental dishonesty be determined, notwithstanding that the notice has not been set aside?

26. ***It appears to me that that gives the court a discretion as to whether to go down this road at all; the court may, following discontinuance, direct that, nevertheless, the costs issues arising out of the allegation of a fundamentally dishonest claim be determined, but it is not obliged to do so. Whether it does so, and in what manner it does so, should be determined in the light of the overriding objective and the considerations of proportionality to which I have referred.***

[…]

28. ***If, however, contrary to those submissions, I were to decide that the issues arising from the fundamental dishonesty allegation should be determined, the next question is essentially one of procedure. Should I deal with that application substantively now on the basis of the materials before me, which are essentially the papers in the case together with a witness statement from the 2nd defendant's solicitor explaining them and putting them in their context, and of course the submissions of counsel? Alternatively, should I give further directions for the manner in which the issue***

> ***should be determined? For example, directions for an oral trial of the kind that I have described.*** *The third question, assuming that I decide to deal with the application now, is what conclusions I should reach as to whether the claimant was dishonest and whether, more particularly, the claim itself was fundamentally dishonest."*

Returning to the issue later in his judgment, HHJ Maloney Q.C. continued (at [52]):

> *"52. No authority was cited to me to support the proposition that before any finding of dishonesty is made, a person must either be heard in oral evidence or at least be given the opportunity to be so heard. It will depend on all of the circumstances, and it will also need to be considered in the context of proportionality. There will be some cases where the evidence is clear and overwhelming, perhaps even the subject of an admission. There will be some cases in which the issue can justly be determined by a limited enquiry. There will be some cases in which the issue can only justly be determined by the hearing of oral evidence and the opportunity of cross-examination. In that situation, the court would then have to consider, going back to the first question that I defined earlier in this judgment, whether it was appropriate and proportionate to pursue that enquiry at all, having in mind the amount of costs at stake."*

In determining the case before him, HHJ Maloney Q.C. considered that the evidence in relation to the Defendant's argument on liability was not so clear that it could justly be determined on the papers without hearing oral evidence and it was not proportionate to have a substantive oral hearing including calling the Claimant and expert witnesses who had opined on the issue. However, the issue in relation to the Claimant's case on quantum was a different matter:

> *"55. Putting all of those together and adopting, I hope, a practical and pragmatic approach to the working of this jurisdiction, it appears to me that I can fairly describe this claimant colloquially as*

> *having being caught "bang to rights". When the court concludes that the surveillance evidence is so strong that the claimant has been caught "bang to rights", then it can properly and proportionately reach a conclusion of dishonesty in the exercise of its costs jurisdiction, without being required either to have an oral hearing, or to give the opportunity of an oral hearing.*
>
> *[…]*
>
> *57. If the courts were too readily persuaded to approach the matter in that disproportionate way* [i.e. the way urged upon the Judge by the Claimant, namely, the need for a further hearing with oral evidence] *then the deterrence of dishonest civil litigation, both as to liability and as to quantum (which it is also a part of social policy to combat and which it is the function of these parts of CPR 44 to deal with) would be rendered ineffective."*

Wayne Rouse v Aviva Insurance (Bradford County Court) (15/1/2016) (HHJ Gosnell)

In *Rouse*, the Claimant discontinued no more than three days before the trial. The Defendant applied for a finding of 'fundamental dishonesty'. HHJ Gosnell observed (at [10]) that:

> *"…it is a matter for the court's discretion as to how this procedure should be adopted. In my view, where the Rules do not say what the procedure should be but direct that issues have to be determined, it is within the court's general discretion how to do that. If it could only be done on paper I would have expected the Rules to say so. Therefore, for the reasons that I indicate, in general terms, the court has the option how to adopt this procedure whether in writing, whether with a limited inquiry or whether with a full trial. In the particular facts of this case it seems to me that either a full trial or a limited inquiry at least giving the claimant and his witness the*

> *opportunity to give evidence is the right and fair way to move forward."*

In *Rouse*, the learned Judge was clearly conscious of the stage in proceedings at which the Notice was served, and the fact that the case was ready for trial:

> *"... I will go back to His Honour Judge Maloney's guidance at paragraph 52 of his judgment and, in my view, given the examples in* [the District Judge's] *judgment, where the case is virtually ready for trial and all the evidence has already been prepared and exchanged, that might be a strong argument for saying that it would be proportionate to have a trial. Where discontinuance was served just after the defence, in my view, that would mean it will be a strong argument not to have a trial for the very reason that* [the District Judge below] *outlined because you would be forcing both parties to do a lot of costly work which would not be required otherwise."* (at [7])

HHJ Gosnell also made the observation that where, at a hearing of a Defendant's application for finding of 'fundamental dishonesty', the Claimant does not give evidence or does not proffer any reason for the decision to discontinue, the Defendant would be entitled to invite the court to draw adverse inferences (at [4]):

> *"If I reach the conclusion that there may have to be a hearing at which parties can give evidence, I think it must be right that where the claimant does not give evidence or does not proffer any reason for the decision to discontinue, then the defendant can invite the court to draw an adverse inference. I think* [Counsel for the Defendant] *is right that no-one can compel a claimant to give evidence in these circumstances and similarly no-one can compel him to explain why he discontinued. However, obviously, for the court to find that notwithstanding the somewhat unusual circumstances and his late discontinuance, he is not dishonest. I think that an explanation for the discontinuance would be very helpful to the court in making that*

conclusion. Therefore, that is why I disagree with that part of the District Judge's judgment."

<u>*Alpha Insurance A/S v (1) Lorraine Roche; (2) Brendan Roche* [2018] EWHC 1342 (QB)</u>

Facts and First Instance Decision

In *Roche,* the claim arose out of road traffic accident on the 6th April 2016. The Defendant/Appellant's insured had collided with a vehicle being driven by the First Claimant/Respondent. It was claimed that the Second Claimant/Respondent was a passenger in the front passenger seat. Both Claimants sought damages for personal injury. The Defendant's Defence admitted breach of duty but alleged that the only occupant of the other vehicle was the First Claimant and that the Second Claimant's claim was fraudulent. It was further alleged that the First Claimant's claim was tainted by dishonesty. The day before trial the Claimants filed a Notice of Discontinuance.

At first instance HHJ Gregory refused to direct that issues arising out of an allegation that the claim was fundamentally dishonesty be determined following the Claimant's service of a Notice of Discontinuance.

The learned Circuit Judge took the view that, "*to set aside and identify a further trial date for the ventilation of that particular isolated issue in this particular case would be, on balance, a disproportionate use of limited and precious court resources, given the amount of time and court resources that have already been devoted to the pursuit of this case. [...] In reality, there are many instances coming before these courts of cases where occupancy, or alleged phantom occupancy, turn out to be not sinister in the least, and certainly, there are reasons for parties discontinuing their litigation on multi-faceted and diverse (sic), and there is nothing, in my judgment, which suggests that there is any particular exceptional quality about this particular case that should cause me to give further directions and to set aside further court time to allow this particular isolated issue of dishonesty to be ventilated."*

Defendant's Argument on Appeal

The Defendant appealed, arguing that the Judge had:

(a) Failed to give any, or any sufficient, weight to the public interest in maintaining the integrity of the legal system and ensuring that dishonest claimants should be exposed as such and pay the costs of litigation;

(b) Placed too much emphasis on the court resources required to determine the issue, and insufficient emphasis on the waste of resources by the Claimant in serving the Notice of Discontinuance at the eleventh hour;

(c) Placed too much weight on general difficulties faced by Defendants in challenging occupancy, and insufficient weight on the substantive allegation and cogency of the evidence in the case;

(d) Placed too much weight upon a general acceptance that reasons for discontinuance are multi-faceted without any explanation being put before the court; and

(e) Placed an unnecessary burden on the defendant to establish a "particular exceptional quality".

Decision of the High Court

Yip J accepted that, on its face, the judgment of HHJ Gregory contained an error of law in that he had applied a test of 'exceptionality' which was not contained in the relevant applicable provision. Accordingly, the appeal was allowed and Yip J had to exercise her discretion afresh.

Yip J confirmed that, the correct approach with regard to the discretion under PD 44, paragraph 12.4(c) was, "*an unfettered one, requiring the weighing of all relevant considerations in accordance with the overriding objective.*" [at 16]. She expressly rejected the suggestion that the test should be analogous to that applied in relation to an application for summary judgment under CPR r. 24.2.

She further clarified that, "*There is no presumption that the court should generally direct determination of the issues of fundamental dishonesty nor is there any presumption that the court should generally not make such a direction. In other words, giving such a direction should be seen to be neither routine nor exceptional.*" [at 17]

Further, Yip J gave guidance that:

> *"18. The provision has been introduced expressly to allow issues of fundamental dishonesty to be determined after discontinuance. Inevitably, this involves the allocation of further court resources to a case in which the claim is no longer being pursued. It will not be uncommon for such cases to involve relatively modest costs. However, in considering proportionality, it does need to be recognised that there is a public interest in identifying false claims and in claimants who pursue such claims being required to meet the costs of the litigation.*
>
> *19. Each case will depend on its own facts. This is an area in which judges sitting at first instance must be afforded a wide margin of appreciation. Provided that the judge has weighed the relevant considerations, an appeal court will not interfere merely because it might have arrived at the opposite conclusion. Appeals against discretionary decisions as to whether it is appropriate for issues relating to fundamental dishonesty to be determined are not to be encouraged."*

When exercising her discretion afresh as to whether to allow the allegation of fundamental dishonesty to be determined, Yip J indicated that two factors weighed "*heavily in the balance*", namely: (i) the very late stage at which the claim was discontinued ["*They had maintained their claim until the very last moment*"] and (ii) the complete absence of an explanation from the claimants for having discontinued. In relation to the latter point, Yip J observed, "*I accept that there may be many reasons why a claimant will discontinue. However, where liability is not disputed save for the allegation of fundamental dishonesty and where the matter is close to trial, I believe some explanation can reasonably be expected.*" (at [27]).

It is clear from the judgment that Yip J also specifically took into account:

(a) The Defendant's evidence raised a triable issue (on occupancy) which was based on evidence that was capable of being accepted (although the Judge felt it was not particularly strong);

(b) The late discontinuance meant that the Defendant had incurred the costs of defending the matter right through to preparation for trial and it had done so on the basis it believed a false claim had been made. There was also consequent inconvenience caused to the Defendant;

(c) Court resources had been allocated for trial;

(d) The Defendant's witnesses were prepared to attend trial and in fact, had done so on the day allocated for the trial; and

(e) The Second Claimant's age. He was still a minor (aged 16) and he may be caused distress if unfounded allegations that he was lying were put to him [although Yip J made it clear that she did not feel that this factor was sufficient to outweigh the factors

> pointing towards allowing the Defendant to litigate the fundamental dishonesty issue].

On balance, Yip J concluded that it was reasonable for the Defendant to be given the opportunity to put forward its evidence and to test the Claimant's evidence on fundamental dishonesty.

CHAPTER TEN
APPLICATIONS TO SET ASIDE A NOTICE OF DISCONTINUANCE

Of course, whilst not essential, it remains open to the Defendant to additionally make an application to set aside the Claimant's Notice of Discontinuance if it wishes to do so. Whilst the law relating to such applications is, strictly speaking, outside the scope of this work, the following is a brief introduction to the relevant Rules and the leading authority.

The Court has the power to set aside a Notice of Discontinuance in accordance with CPR r. 38.4:

> *"Right to apply to have notice of discontinuance set aside*
>
> ***38.4***
>
> *(1) Where the claimant discontinues under rule 38.2(1) the defendant may apply to have the notice of discontinuance set aside(GL).*
>
> *(2) The defendant may not make an application under this rule more than 28 days after the date when the notice of discontinuance was served on him."*

The commentary in the White Book confirms that the Court is to approach such applications on the basis that it has a discretion which should be exercised to give effect to the Overriding Objective of dealing with cases justly and at proportionate cost. An abuse of the Court's process would be a powerful factor in favour of granting the application but abuse is neither a necessary or exclusive criterion which must be satisfied in order for an application to succeed.

The leading authority in relation to setting aside a Notice of Discontinuance remains the *High Commissioner for Pakistan in the United Kingdom v National Westminster Bank* [2015] EWHC 55 (Ch). In summary, the High Court has confirmed that the following principles apply to such an application:

(a) CPR r. 38.4(1) must be construed, and the discretion under it exercised, with the aim of furthering the overriding objective (at [40]).

(b) Henderson J stated that: "*Thus I consider that the court should approach an application to set aside a notice of discontinuance under rule 38.4(1) on the basis that the court has a discretion which it should exercise with the aim of giving effect to the overriding objective of dealing with the case justly and at proportionate cost. If the facts disclose an abuse of the court's process, that will no doubt continue to be a powerful factor in favour of granting the application; but it would in my view be wrong to treat abuse of process as either a necessary or an exclusive criterion which has to be satisfied if the application is to succeed*" (at [46]).

(c) Henderson J agreed (at [47]) with the comments of Aikens J (as he then was) in *Sheltam Rail Co Ltd v Mirambo Holdings Ltd* [2008] EWHC 829 (Comm), in particular where Aikens J said: "*When considering whether or not a notice of discontinuance constitutes an abuse of the process of the court, I regard a useful question to ask (as under the old RSC) if the permission of the court had been required to issue a notice of discontinuance, would that permission have been granted unconditionally? However, that it not the only matter to consider before a court exercises its discretion to set aside a notice of discontinuance under CPR r 38.4. A court must also be entitled to consider both the circumstances in which the notice of discontinuance was issued and what the claimant is attempting to achieve by issuing and serving the notice*".

CHAPTER ELEVEN THE DECISION IN MABB V ENGLISH

ng the additional head of liability may confer no additional benefit but No consideration of the interaction between a Claimant's right to discontinue and the continuing application of QOCS would be complete without touching briefly on the decision of Mrs Justice May DBE in *Mabb v English* [2017] EWHC 3616 (QB).

Whilst *Mabb* dealt with the exception to QOCS contained in CPR r. 44.15 (i.e. striking the claim out) and is therefore not a case dealing directly with the 'fundamental dishonesty' exception contained in CPR r. 44.16(1), it is suggested that the dicta of Her Ladyship are likely to be some considerable force when considering an application for a finding of 'fundamental dishonesty' post discontinuance, whether in the context of a complementary application to set aside a Notice of Discontinuance, or not.

In *Mabb* it was held that, on the facts, and in the absence of fraud, there was no inherent unfairness in a Claimant filing a Notice of Discontinuance in a personal injury action so as to avoid the effect of CPR r. 44.15. The Court found that the exception to QOCS would continue to apply. Importantly, May J said:

> 33. *"[...] there is nothing inherently abusive or contrary to the overriding objective in a party taking steps to avoid a costs liability.*
>
> 34. *The problem for* [Counsel for the Defendant's] *argument is that there is no rule preventing a claimant with QOCS protection from taking steps to secure the benefit of that protection whilst it still exists. CPR r.38 does provide for some restrictions on the right of a claimant to discontinue. The court's permission is required, for*

instance, where an interim injunction has been issued. Nothing is said in the rule about discontinuance in the context of QOCS, nor is there any provision in Part 44 itself, although there is provision, in r.44.16, for permission of the court to be sought for a costs order to be enforced where a claim has been fraudulently (as opposed to merely incompetently) pursued.

35. *Accordingly, whilst I can see that the effect of r.38 and 44.15 taken together can give rise to a situation in which a defendant, as here, loses the opportunity to obtain the benefit of the exception, I cannot conclude that there is any inherent unfairness in a claimant taking advantage of the result that the rules together permit, at least in their current form. I would not rule out the possibility of a case falling short of fraud in which the behaviour of a claimant or their solicitors might on the facts be so egregious or cynical as to justify setting aside a Notice of Discontinuance in accordance with the overriding objection, but this case is not so extreme as to lead me to that conclusion. The conduct of these proceedings on behalf of the claimant does appear to have been dilatory and lacking in many respects, but not to the extent that requires me to reinstate proceedings by setting aside the Notice of Discontinuance. Accordingly, I decline to do so."*

CHAPTER TWELVE
PRACTICE POINTS

When considering applications for a finding of 'fundamental dishonesty' following the service of a Notice of Discontinuance practitioners may want to bear in mind the following points:

(a) In the vast majority of cases applications for the determination of alleged dishonesty issues in accordance with PD 44, paragraph 12.4(c) should be made *in conjunction with* an application to set aside the Notice in accordance with r. 38.4. There is little, if any, disadvantage in making the applications in tandem. Whilst the application to set aside the Notice requires the Court to additionally consider the dicta in the *High Commissioner for Pakistan* case and, to that extent, creates an additional hurdle over which the Defendant is required to jump, it is highly likely that where the evidence and the circumstances of a case are sufficient for one application to succeed, so too will the other;

(b) The closer to trial that the Claimant files a Notice of Discontinuance, the more likely it is that the Court will accede to a request to determine dishonesty issues. Conversely, the earlier in the proceedings the Notice is filed, the less likely it is that the Court will allow those issues to be aired by any method;

(c) The absence of an explanation from the Claimant as to the reason(s) for the discontinuance is likely to be an important factor. The closer to trial the Notice is served, the more important this factor becomes. It is likely to be highly relevant in cases where breach of duty is admitted and the allegations of dishonesty relate to other matters, such as occupancy, or quantum;

(d) If a Claimant files a Notice of Discontinuance shortly before the trial it is more likely that a Judge will agree to determining allegations of 'fundamental dishonesty' at a further hearing at which evidence is called and tested [the vast majority of the preparation for trial already having been completed, and the bulk of the costs already incurred];

(e) It is crucial to objectively assess the merits of the dishonesty allegations in the context of the evidence *already available* at the time the Claimant files the Notice of Discontinuance. If there is clear and objective evidence of dishonesty, for example, social media searches; compelling forensic engineering evidence; covert surveillance etc., such evidence may well be sufficient to persuade a Judge to make a finding of dishonesty without a need to hear oral evidence. If the Court's determination of the dishonesty issue is likely to turn, to a large degree, on an assessment of competing witness evidence, a Judge is less likely to allow the issue to proceed to a determination. A Judge is highly unlikely to permit the determination of dishonesty issues where it appears on the evidence currently available the Defendant's case is objectively weak and is reliant on further helpful evidence being elicited during cross-examination;

(f) The amount at stake in terms of costs is likely to be an important factor, particularly when compared with the additional costs to be incurred in relation to whatever method of determination is proposed. A Defendant should be able to demonstrate the costs position in relation to both issues, in order to assist and persuade the Judge to allow it to proceed;

(g) Knowledge of your Judge may be helpful, for example, whether he/she has a reputation for being particularly lenient, or particularly exacting, in relation to issues of dishonesty. Counsel's input can be useful in this regard;

(h) There has to be a sense of realism when deciding whether or not to pursue an application for a finding of dishonesty post discontinuance – the Court has a wide discretion which is unlikely to be susceptible to an appeal. The prospects of succeeding with the application need to be carefully scrutinised. Simply because a Claimant has discontinued, does not axiomatically mean they are dishonest. In some cases, particularly those where there are live issues on liability and the Court's determination of any alleged dishonesty issues will turn on the performance of the Claimant in the witness box [something which is clearly not ascertainable by the Defendant in advance of the trial] the filing of a Notice of Discontinuance can, and should, be seen as a victory. Any pressure which the Defendant has exerted (whether in correspondence or otherwise) has resulted in the Claimant abandoning the claim, which brings with it consequent costs savings;

(i) An over-optimistic or poorly prepared application for a finding of 'fundamental dishonesty', which is ultimately unsuccessful, will be penalised in costs, quite possibly on the indemnity basis. There is a risk, therefore, that any costs savings secured as a result of the Claimant filing a Notice of Discontinuance are wiped out, by the costs order made on the subsequent application;

(j) It is vital to remember that the Court has a discretion as to *how* the process of determination takes place. Any application for a finding of dishonesty has to be realistic and pitched appropriately. If the Claimant discontinues after the Defence is filed, save in an exceptional case, the Court is simply not going to require the parties to proceed through the disclosure exercise, prepare witness statements etc., in order to have a full trial. To do so would be grossly disproportionate. It is suggested that a Judge is more likely to exercise the first limb of their discretion to allow the issue to proceed to a determination if the method of determination proposed is sensible and proportionate. An important caveat arises – any Defendant must first be satisfied that they do, in fact, have reasonable prospects of being able to subsequently prove dishonesty through the medium of the enquiry proposed. There is, for example, simply no point in proposing a paper-based enquiry when the documentary evidence alone is too weak to establish dishonesty;

(k) Where a decision is taken to make an application for a finding of 'fundamental dishonesty' post discontinuance, the application must be made promptly. A Judge will look highly critically on a delayed application, not least because of concerns that a Claimant would be made to face serious allegations which may have become 'stale' and arise some time after the claim has actually been brought to an end, and on account of the perceived benefit in the finality of litigation;

(l) The Claimant's right to discontinue their claim at any time has not, in any way, been eroded by the implementation of QOCS. The interplay between discontinuance, the automatic costs order in the Defendant's favour, and the *prima facie* unenforceable nature of that costs order, is the intended consequence of the various Rules in play.

SECTION (IV)

APPLICABLE COSTS ASSESSMENT PROVISIONS

CHAPTER THIRTEEN
COSTS PROVISIONS

The overwhelming majority of cases in which 'fundamental dishonesty' issues arise will be proceeding on the Fast and Multi Tracks by reason of the likely value of the personal injury element of the claim. It is not, however, impossible that a claim to which the QOCS provisions applies may be proceeding on the Small Claims Track. Where a Defendant is able to successfully establish 'fundamental dishonesty', actual assessment of the costs to which the Defendant will be entitled (all other things being equal) will be determined in accordance with the following provisions.

(i) Small Claims Case

Costs in a small claim case are determined in accordance with CPR r. 27.14, which sets out a highly prescriptive regime of *inter partes* recoverable costs. In short, the default position in a small claims track case is that the Defendant will not recover any of its' costs of defending the claim, save and to the extent that it can satisfy the "*unreasonable behaviour*" test set out in r. 27.14(2)(g):

> *"Costs on the small claims track*
>
> *27.14*
>
> *(1) This rule applies to any case which has been allocated to the small claims track .*
>
> *(Rules 46.11 and 46.13 make provision in relation to orders for costs made before a claim has been allocated to the small claims track)*
>
> *(2) The court may not order a party to pay a sum to another party in respect of that other party's costs, fees and expenses, including those relating to an appeal, except –*

> *[…]*
>
> *(g) such further costs as the court may assess by the summary procedure and order to be paid by a party who has behaved unreasonably"*

It is suggested that where the Defendant is able to satisfy the Court that the criteria in CPR r. 44.16(1) is met, that will be sufficient to satisfy the exception in r. 27.14(2)(g) to enable the Defendant to obtain a summarily assessed award of costs. Indeed, it is suggested that it would be perverse for the Court to find that the Claimant had been dishonest in a way that was fundamental but not go on to then find that he/she had behaved unreasonably. Such costs will be assessed on normal summary assessment principles. Given the proven dishonesty, there would be a cogent argument for such costs to be assessed on the indemnity basis.

<u>(ii) Fast Track Cases</u>

In relation to cases proceeding on the Fast Track there are two possible scenarios:

(a) Those cases which initially fell within the scope of, and proceeded in accordance with:

   i. The "Pre-Action Protocol for Low Value Personal Injury Claims in Road Traffic Accidents";

   ii. The "Pre-Action Protocol for Low Value Personal Injury (Employers' Liability) Claims"; or

   iii. The "Pre-Action Protocol for Resolution of Package Travel Claims"

   [hereafter collectively referred to as the "fixed costs claims"] which, for whatever reason, have ceased to continue under the relevant process and Part 7 proceedings have been issued; and

(b) Those cases which did not proceed in accordance with any of the above portal schemes.

(a) 'Fixed Costs Claims'

By reason of CPR r. 45.29A, such claims are subject to the now well-known fixed recoverable costs regime set out in Section IIIA to Part 45. The regime itself prescribes what is to happen in a situation where the Court has made a finding that the claim is 'fundamentally dishonest'. In relation to fixed cost claims, the relevant provision is r. 45.29F which, so far as is material, provides:

> *"Defendants' costs*
>
> *45.29F*
>
> *(1) In this rule—*
>
> *[...]*
>
> *(b) paragraph (10) applies to assessments to which the exclusions from qualified one way costs shifting in rules 44.15 and 44.16 apply; and*
>
> *[...]*
>
> *(10) Where, in a case to which this Section applies, any of the exceptions to qualified one way costs shifting in rules 44.15 and 44.16 is established, the court will assess the defendant's costs without reference to this rule."*

Accordingly, the fixed costs regime ceases to apply, and the Defendant is entitled to a summary assessment of costs, on normal principles. Given the proven dishonesty, there would be a cogent argument for such costs to be assessed on the indemnity basis.

(b) All Other Cases

Whilst the overwhelming majority of personal injury cases which proceed on the Fast Track will fall within the ambit of one of the three Pre-Action Protocols referred to above, it is still possible that a claim may not do so (although such cases are likely to be rare).

In such circumstances, given the Court is not bound by the application of a fixed costs regime, at the conclusion of a trial where 'fundamental dishonesty' is established, the Judge would simply make a summary assessment of costs in the Defendant's favour, applying normal principles. Given the proven dishonesty, there would be a cogent argument for such costs to be assessed on the indemnity basis.

(iii) Multi-Track

Notwithstanding repeated suggestions that they may be forthcoming in the not too distant future, as at the time of writing, fixed costs have not been implemented in relation to cases proceeding on the Multi-Track and thus, at the conclusion of a trial where 'fundamental dishonesty' is established, the Judge would simply make a summary assessment of costs in the Defendant's favour, applying normal principles. Given the proven dishonesty, there would be a cogent argument for such costs to be assessed on the indemnity basis.

SECTION (V)

SECTION 57 OF THE CRIMINAL JUSTICE AND COURTS ACT 2015

CHAPTER FOURTEEN
ORIGINS OF THE PROVISION – THE DECISION IN SUMMERS V FAIRCLOUGH HOMES

In order to understand the origins and intentions of s. 57 of the 2015 Act, one first has to understand the perceived 'problem' that it was enacted specifically to address. Thus, one must consider the Supreme Court's decision in *Summers v Fairclough Homes Limited* [2012] UKSC 26, and the state of the law following that judgment.

Summers v Fairclough Homes Limited [2012] UKSC 26

The Issue

The issue before the Supreme Court was neatly summarised by Lord Clarke in the judgment's opening paragraph where he identified it as (at [1)]:

> "*whether a civil court ("the court") has power to strike out a statement of case as an abuse of process after a trial at which the court has held that the defendant is liable in damages to the claimant in an ascertained sum and, if so, in what circumstances such a power should be exercised. The driving force behind the appeal is the defendant's liability insurers, who say that fraudulent claims of the kind found to exist here are rife and should in principle be struck out as an abuse of the court's process under CPR 3.4(2) or under the inherent jurisdiction of the court.*"

The Facts and First Instance Judgment

On the 13th May 2003, while employed by the Defendant, Mr Summers was injured in an accident at work when he fell from a stacker truck, suffering a fractured scaphoid in his right hand and a comminuted fracture of his left calcaneum. The Defendant initially admitted liability but, after receipt of the Claimant's medical records which appeared to cast doubt on the Claimant's account of the accident, the Defendant successfully applied to withdraw that admission. The matter went to trial and the Claimant was successful on liability, with damages to be assessed at a later date.

On the 4th October 2007, just over five weeks after the liability trial, the Defendant obtained covert surveillance evidence of the Claimant. The Claimant signed a witness statement on the 5th October 2007 which included an assertion that he was not able to stand for more than 10 – 15 minutes. The Defendant continued to subject the Claimant to surveillance. The parties' orthopaedic experts met and prepared a joint statement, without sight of the footage. The Claimant served his first schedule of loss totalling £838,616. The Defendant disclosed the surveillance evidence and served a re-amended Defence alleging that the claim was grossly and dishonestly exaggerated, and asserted that it should be struck out in its entirety. Shortly after receipt of the re-amended Defence, the Claimant made a Part 36 offer of £190,200.

The orthopaedic experts met again and prepared a second report, having seen the surveillance. The Department of Work and Pensions also subsequently disclosed surveillance showing the Claimant apparently working without difficulty in 2009.

In June 2008 the Claimant served a second Schedule of Loss, totalling £250,923 and made a further offer to settle of £150,000. The Defendant declined to attend a Joint Settlement Meeting. In December 2009 the Claimant served his third Schedule of Loss, totalling £251,481. That claim was maintained at trial.

The trial Judge rejected the Claimant's assertion that he had suffered with significant ongoing disability. The Judge rejected what the Claimant had told his treating doctors and the medical experts as to his ongoing symptoms on the basis that: (i) what was seen on the surveillance was absolutely inconsistent with such disabilities; it was also inconsistent with what was contained on the DWP application form; (ii) the claimant's attempt to explain the footage on the basis that he was on strong painkillers at the time was not credible, particularly when he was seen on two occasions going two and from two separate medical experts' consulting rooms without crutches when leaving and returning home, but using crutches when entering and leaving the doctor's premises; and (iii) his wife's diary, which contained evidence of him working and playing football, belied any protestation of ongoing symptoms.

The Judge concluded that:

> *"57. The evidence before me is sufficiently cogent to sustain a claim of fraud not only applying the civil standard of being satisfied on the balance of probabilities but also on the criminal standard of being satisfied beyond reasonable doubt insofar as that standard is materially different when allegations of fraud are made. In my judgment the Claimant has deliberately lied to the medical men and to the Department of Work and Pensions on the application form when he said he had ongoing symptoms after March 2007. The Claimant was clearly able to work without difficulty or pain when filmed in October 2007 driving and loading a van with kitchen fitting components and again in 2009 when filmed with the mobile food van. His wife's diary confirms he was working at various other times. I can only infer he was working for reward; the diary confirms such a conclusion; the explanations of helping out for free, of pushing himself and of learning the business of a mobile food van with a view to purchase is deliberate falsehood and an attempt to explain away what cannot be explained away…"*

The Judge also rejected the assertion that a third arthrodesis which the Claimant had undergone was attributable to the accident, it was not, it was attributable to the Claimant's lies which he told to his treating doctor. The Judge stated, "*The Claimant has got stuck with his own lie; had he told the truth he would be admitting this claim is grossly exaggerated and that he has been claiming benefits under false pretences; this he is not prepared to do as is evidenced by his testimony before me, false as I find, that he is still in pain and needing to use crutches.*"

In total, the trial Judge awarded the Claimant £88,716.76, comprising £18,500 for general damages; £63,776.76 for past loss of earnings; £5,400 for past care and assistance; and £1,400 for 'other services'. A claim for future loss of earnings based on the prospect of promotion was rejected on the basis the Claimant's evidence was unreliable. So too, a claim for a *Smith v Manchester* award was dismissed.

The Defendant argued that the Court had the power to strike out the claim on the basis that it was tainted by fraud and was an abuse of process and that the cases of *Ul-Haq v Shah* [2009] EWCA Civ 542, and *Widlake v BAA Limited* [2009] EWCA Civ 1256 (both Court of Appeal authority on this issue) were wrongly decided. It was accepted that both those cases were binding on the Judge and he accordingly followed them. However, the Judge gave permission to appeal on the basis that there was a real prospect the Supreme Court would take a different view to that taken by the Court of Appeal in those two earlier cases. The Judge envisaged the Court of Appeal refusing the appeal, leaving the Defendant to argue the matter before the Supreme Court.

At the same hearing the Judge heard argument on interest and costs, and considered an application by the Defendant for permission to commence contempt proceedings against the Claimant. The Supreme Court considered that the Judge's decisions in those respects, which were not challenged on appeal in the Court of Appeal or in the Supreme Court, were of "*some significant importance*" in resolving the issues on appeal.

In relation to interest, the Defendant argued that no interest should be awarded on damages after the 30th June 2007, the date by which the

Judge had found the Claimant was fit and should have gone back to work. The Judge accepted the Defendant's submissions that the Claimant had lied about the extent of his injuries, his ability to work, and his need for care and assistance, but nevertheless awarded interest over the whole period, noting that the Defendant had not made a Part 36 offer to protect itself; had refused to attend a JSM; and was not willing to negotiate because it wanted more out of the litigation than a settlement, in particular, it wanted an opportunity to persuade the Supreme Court to strike out the whole claim. The Judge found that the Claimant's lies as to continuing disability did not affect the Defendant's attitude to negotiation or settlement.

In relation to costs, the Defendant's primary argument was that the Claimant should pay all of the Defendant's costs from the date of the judgment on liability. In the alternative, that there should be no order for costs on the basis that the Claimant's fraudulent conduct had increased the costs. The Judge ordered the Defendant to pay the Claimant's costs up to February 2008 [approximately 4 months after surveillance started] save that the Claimant was to pay the Defendant's costs of obtaining the surveillance; and no order for costs after March 2008. The Judge's reasons for so deciding were: if the Claimant had 'come clean' there would have been an earlier trial on quantum; he had persisted in his lies up to, and at, trial; however, by October 2007 the Defendant knew that the Claimant was grossly exaggerating his disability. Whilst it was understandable that the Defendant would wish to obtain further evidence to demonstrate the claimant's falsity, rather than prematurely disclose what it had discovered, it could also be argued that the Defeat should have disclosed the video evidence earlier than January 2009. Also, although the Claimant wanted to negotiate, the Defendant did not want to let the Claimant off the hook once the surveillance was disclosed, because it wanted to obtain an advancement in the law. The Judge observed that the Defendant was not deflected from ascertaining the true position by the Claimant's continued lies – they saw through them. The Defendant was not fooled by the

Claimant's dishonesty. The Defendant chose not to make any offers and, thereby, caused the proceedings to take longer to come to trial.

As to the application for committal for contempt of Court, the Judge held that there was a strong *prima facie* case for believing that the Defendant would be able to show that the claimant was guilty of contempt to the criminal standard. The Judge held that the same was true of the offences of perverting the course of justice, and obtaining property or a pecuniary advantage by deception. However, the Judge held that it was not in the public interest for permission for contempt proceedings to be given, and he declined to do so.

The Court of Appeal

The Court of Appeal held that they were bound by *Ul-Haq* and *Widlake* to hold that the Court had no power to strike out the claim in its entirety. It refused permission to appeal, which was later granted by the Supreme Court.

Arguments to the Supreme Court

Before the Supreme Court the Defendant argued that the Court had the power, either pursuant to CPR r. 3.4(2) or its inherent jurisdiction, to strike out the claim. The Claimant argued that (i) on the basis of *Ul-Haq* and *Widlake*, there was no power to strike the claim out; in the alternative (ii) it would be wrong in principle for the court to strike the claim out after a trial at which the Court had found a Defendant is liable to a Claimant in an ascertained sum; or in the further alternative (iii) on the facts of this case, it should not be struck out.

Decision of the Supreme Court

The Supreme Court held, contrary to the decisions in *Ul-Haq* and *Widlake*, that a Court did have jurisdiction to strike out a statement of case under CPR r. 3.4(2) or its inherent jurisdiction on the ground that there was an abuse of the Court's process, even after the trial of an action in circumstances where the Court had been able to make a proper assessment of both liability and quantum. However, for many of the reasons expounded by the Court of Appeal in those earlier authorities, the Supreme Court held that,

> "*...as a matter of principle, it should only do so* [strike out] *in very exceptional circumstances*" (at [33]).

The Court noted that the approach in *Ul-Haq*, which had been followed in *Widlake*, was somewhat different from the approach taken by the Court of Appeal in the case of *Masood v Zahoor* [2009] EWCA Civ 650 where it was accepted that, at least theoretically, it would have been open to the trial judge, even at the conclusion of the hearing, to strike the claim out.

The Supreme Court considered:

(a) The language of CPR r. 3.4 supported the existence of a jurisdiction to strike out a claim for abuse of process, even where to do so would defeat a substantive claim. Deliberately to make a false claim and to adduce false evidence is an abuse of process. There was nothing in the rule itself to qualify the power. It does not limit the time when such an application can be made, nor does it restrict the circumstances in which it can be made. The only restrictions were in CPR r. 1.1 and 1.2 that the Court must decide cases in accordance with the overriding objective, which was to do so justly;

(b) Under the CPR the court had a wide discretion as to how its powers should be exercised. So, whilst it had the power to strike out, it had a wide discretion as to which of its many powers to exercise. The same was true in relation to the Court's inherent jurisdiction;

(c) Importantly, in agreeing with *Masood,* the Supreme Court stated that, "*... while the court has power to strike a claim out at the end of a trial, it would only do so if it were satisfied that the party's abuse of process was such that he had thereby forfeited the right to have his claim determined*" (at [43]). It would be a very rare case where, at the end of trial, it would be appropriate for a Judge to strike out a case rather than dismiss it in a judgment on the merits in the usual way. The same was true where the court was able to assess the both the liability of the Defendant and the amount of that liability; and

(d) It rejected the Claimant's suggestion that an ascertained claim for damages could only be removed by Parliament, and not by the Courts. It was for the Court, not Parliament, to protect the Court's process. The power to strike out was not a power to punish, but to protect the Court's process.

The Supreme Court held that it was in the public interest that there should be a power to strike out a statement of case for abuse of process, both under the inherent jurisdiction and the CPR, but that in deciding whether or not to exercise the power, the court must examine the circumstances of the case scrupulously in order to ensure that to strike out the claim was a proportionate means of achieving the aim of controlling the process of the Court and deciding cases justly.

In considering how the power should be exercised, the Supreme Court reiterated the wide discretion afforded to the Court as to how to exercise its case management powers and stated (at [49]) (emphasis supplied):

> *"The draconian step of striking a claim out is always a last resort, a fortiori where to do so would deprive the claimant of a substantive right to which the court had held that he was entitled after a fair trial.* ***It is very difficult indeed to think of circumstances in which such a conclusion would be proportionate****. Such circumstances*

> *might, however, include a case where there had been a massive attempt to deceive the court but the award of damages would be very small."*

The Defendant argued that it was necessary to strike out the claim in circumstances of this kind, in order to deter fraudulent claims of the type made as they are all too prevalent. The Supreme Court accepted that all reasonable steps should be taken to deter such cases, but that there was a balance to be struck. To date, that balance had been struck by assessing both liability and quantum and providing those assessments could be carried out fairly, in giving judgment in the ordinary way. The Court stated that, "*We accept that such an approach will be correct in the vast majority of cases*" (at [51]). The Court did not accept that unless claims were struck out, dishonest claimants would not be deterred. There were other methods of achieving deterrence, including: ensuring the dishonesty does not increase the award of damages; making orders for costs; reducing interest; and proceedings for contempt of court and/or criminal proceedings.

The Court reiterated that:

> *"61. The test in every case must be what is just and proportionate. It seems to us that it will only be in the very exceptional case that it will be just and proportionate for the court to strike out an action after a trial. The more appropriate course in the civil proceedings will be that proposed in both Masood v Zahoor and Ul-Haq v Shah. Judgment will be given on the claim if the claimant's case is established on the facts. All proper inferences can be drawn against the claimant. The claimant may be held entitled to some costs but is likely to face a substantial order for indemnity costs in respect of time wasted by his fraudulent claims. The defendant may well be able to protect itself against costs by making a Calderbank offer. Moreover, it is open to the defendant (or its insurer) to seek to bring contempt proceedings against the claimant, which are likely to result in the imprisonment of the claimant if they are successful. It seems to us that*

> *the combination of these consequences is like to be a very effective deterrent to claimants bringing dishonest or fraudulent claims, especially if (as should of course happen in appropriate cases) the risks are explained by the claimant's solicitor. It further seems to us that it is in principle more appropriate to penalise such a claimant as a contemnor than to relieve the defendant of what the court has held to be a substantive liability."*

Notwithstanding the Court's acceptance that this was a "*serious case of abuse of process*", on its facts, the Court declined to strike out, considering it neither proportionate nor just to do so, and therefore wrong in principle.

<u>Comment</u>

Summers was, on any assessment, an extreme level of dishonesty. The trial Judge considered it sufficient to maintain a plea of fraud to the criminal standard of proof and observed that there was a strong *prima facie* case for believing that the Defendant would be able to show that the claimant was guilty of contempt of Court; perverting the course of justice; and obtaining property or a pecuniary advantage by deception. The Supreme Court called the Claimant's claim a "*...serious case of abuse of process*". Yet, notwithstanding the Supreme Court's confirmation that, as a matter of law, the Court retained a power to strike out even after trial, it declined to do so on the facts of the case, considering strike out to be unjust and disproportionate.

The Supreme Court held that strike out after trial would only be appropriate in "*very exceptional circumstances*" and further that it was "*... very difficult indeed to think of circumstances in which* [the conclusion to strike out] *would be proportionate.*"

Following the Supreme Court's judgment an obvious question arose – if the extreme level of proven dishonesty in *Summers* was insufficient to warrant a strike out of the claim post trial, in what circumstances could the power ever actually be used lawfully? Although the Supreme Court had confirmed beyond doubt that such a power existed, at the same time as doing so it practically divested that power of any meaningful effect and essentially resigned it to obscurity through setting what appeared to be an unachievably high threshold which a case would need to meet, in order for the power to be invoked.

CHAPTER FIFTEEN
THE RELEVANT STATUTORY PROVISIONS AND PARLIAMENTARY COMMENTARY

The legal position post- *Summers v Fairclough* was clearly considered unacceptable and undesirable by Parliament, who intervened in passing s. 57 of the Criminal Justice and Courts Act 2015. In doing so, Parliament, essentially reversed the position as it stood post- *Summers.*

Section 57 came into force on the 13th April 2015 and applies to proceedings issued on, or after, that date (s. 57(9)).

It is worth setting the section out in full. It provides as follows:

> ***57 Personal injury claims: cases of fundamental dishonesty***
>
> *(1) This section applies where, in proceedings on a claim for damages in respect of personal injury ("the primary claim")—*
>
>> *(a) the court finds that the claimant is entitled to damages in respect of the claim, but*
>>
>> *(b) on an application by the defendant for the dismissal of the claim under this section, the court is satisfied on the balance of probabilities that the claimant has been fundamentally dishonest in relation to the primary claim or a related claim.*
>
> *(2) The court must dismiss the primary claim, unless it is satisfied that the claimant would suffer substantial injustice if the claim were dismissed.*

(3) The duty under subsection (2) includes the dismissal of any element of the primary claim in respect of which the claimant has not been dishonest.

(4) The court's order dismissing the claim must record the amount of damages that the court would have awarded to the claimant in respect of the primary claim but for the dismissal of the claim.

(5) When assessing costs in the proceedings, a court which dismisses a claim under this section must deduct the amount recorded in accordance with subsection (4) from the amount which it would otherwise order the claimant to pay in respect of costs incurred by the defendant.

(6) If a claim is dismissed under this section, subsection (7) applies to —

(a) any subsequent criminal proceedings against the claimant in respect of the fundamental dishonesty mentioned in subsection (1)(b), and

(b) any subsequent proceedings for contempt of court against the claimant in respect of that dishonesty.

(7) If the court in those proceedings finds the claimant guilty of an offence or of contempt of court, it must have regard to the dismissal of the primary claim under this section when sentencing the claimant or otherwise disposing of the proceedings.

(8) In this section —

"claim" includes a counter-claim and, accordingly, "claimant" includes a counter-claimant

and "defendant" includes a defendant to a counterclaim; "personal injury" includes any disease and any other impairment of a person's physical or mental condition;

> *"related claim" means a claim for damages in respect of personal injury which is made—*
>
> > *(a) in connection with the same incident or series of incidents in connection with which the primary claim is made, and*
> >
> > *(b) by a person other than the person who made the primary claim.*
>
> *(9) This section does not apply to proceedings started by the issue of a claim form before the day on which this section comes into force."*

It is interesting to note the Government's view of the legislation as it passed through Parliament. Lord Faulks Q.C., the Minister of State for Justice at the time, said at the Committee stage of the passage of the Bill in the House of Lords (Hansard, 23 July 2014, cols 1267 – 1268) (emphasis added):

> *"I am grateful for some of the constructive suggestions that have been made about how the clause ought best to have been drafted. At the moment, it requires the court to dismiss in its entirety any personal injury claim when it is satisfied on the balance of probabilities that the claimant has been fundamentally dishonest, unless it would cause substantial injustice to the claimant to do so. That is of particular relevance when the claimant has grossly exaggerated his claim, and in cases where the claimant has colluded with another person in a fraudulent claim relating to the same incident—also, sadly, a far too common feature of the whole claims industry at the moment.*
>
> *This is part of a series of measures taken by the Government to discourage fraudulent and exaggerated claims, which arise often in motor accident cases and so-called "trips and slips" claims. Such claims cause substantial harm to society as a whole, not least in increasing the insurance premiums that motorists have to pay ...*
>
> ***Under the current law, the courts have discretion to dismiss a claim in cases of dishonesty, but will do so only in very exceptional***

circumstances, and will generally still award the claimant compensation in relation to the "genuine" element of the claim. The Government simply do not believe that people who behave in a fundamentally dishonest way—and I will come to address the adverb in a moment— by grossly exaggerating their own claim or colluding should be allowed to benefit by getting compensation in spite of their deceit. Clause 45 seeks to strengthen the law so that dismissal of the entire claim should become the norm in such cases. *However, at the same time, it recognises that the dismissal of the claim will not always be appropriate and gives the court the discretion not to do so where it would cause substantial injustice to the claimant. To that extent, some of the remarks of my noble friend Lord Marks were entirely apposite. The clause gives the court some flexibility to ensure that the provision is applied fairly and proportionately.*

...

I assure the Committee that the way that the clause is drafted should not result in the courts using the measures lightly. *Civil courts do not make findings of dishonesty lightly in any event; clear evidence is required. The sanction imposed by the clause—the denial of compensation to which the claimant would otherwise be entitled—is a serious one and will be imposed only where the dishonesty is fundamental; that is, where it goes to the heart of the claim. That was very much what my noble friend said about what it was aimed at.*

Of course, "fundamental" has an echo in the Civil Procedure Rules and the qualified, one-way costs shifting. An adverb to qualify a concept such as dishonesty is not linguistically attractive, but if we ask a jury to decide a question such as dishonesty, or ask a judge to decide whether someone has been fundamentally dishonest, it is well within the capacity of any judge. They will know exactly what the clause is aimed at—not the minor inaccuracy about bus fares or the like, but something that goes to the heart. I do not suggest that it wins many prizes for elegance, but it sends the right message to the judge".

CHAPTER SIXTEEN
INTRODUCTION

A number of preliminary observations as to the drafting of s. 57 can be made:

(a) The section **only** applies, where the Claimant is entitled to damages (s. 57(1)(a)). Thus, the section is of no application whatsoever where a claim has been dismissed on its merits;

(b) The Defendant must make an application to invoke the statutory provision (s. 57(1)(b)). There is no suggestion in the Act (and no authority to support the proposition) that the Court is, itself, under a duty to invoke s. 57;

(c) The standard of proof to be applied is the balance of probabilities (s. 57(1)(b));

(d) The relevant dishonesty to be considered by the Court is that of ***the claimant*** (him or herself) and ***not*** the claim (s. 57(1)(b)). This is a crucial distinction as between CPR r. 44.16(1) and s. 57;

(e) The section is engaged where the Claimant's dishonesty goes to the "*primary claim*" i.e. the Claimant's own claim; or a "*related claim*" (s. 57(1)(b)). A "*related claim*" is, in short, either (i) a claim made in connection with the same incident or series of incidents in connection with which the primary claim is made; or (ii) a claim by a person other than the person making the primary claim (as defined in s. 57(8)). Accordingly, the section applies where the Claimant supports a false claim brought by another; the most obvious and perhaps most commonly encountered example will be where the Claimant asserts his/her friend/relative was present in a vehicle at the time of an accident and also sustained injury, and the Court finds as a fact that the friend/relative were not so present;

(f) Where dishonesty is proven the Court **must** dismiss the whole of the claim (s. 57(2)) including any genuine elements (s. 57(3)), subject to it finding that in doing so the Claimant would suffer "substantial injustice". The default position is therefore that the entirety of the claim will be dismissed; whether to dismiss the claim or not it is not an exercise of judicial discretion; and

(g) After dismissing the claim, the Court must assess the quantum of damages of the "genuine" part(s) of the claim (s. 57(4)). The purpose of so doing is so that the sum of damages the Claimant would have been awarded but for the dismissal under s. 57 (the "genuine" element) can be deducted from the amount that the Court assesses the Defendant is entitled to by way of costs in a 'setting-off process'. That process yields the sum the Claimant will actually be ordered to pay (s. 57(5)). The process can perhaps best be expressed through the following 'formula':

Costs awarded to the Defendant following assessment – Quantum of genuine element(s) of the claim = sum actually payable by the Claimant to the Defendant.

CHAPTER SEVENTEEN
THE DECISION IN LONDON ORGANISING COMMITTEE OF THE OLYMPIC & PARALYMPIC GAMES (IN LIQUIDATION) V HAYDN SINFIELD

Issues surrounding the interpretation of s. 57 of the 2015 Act and how it should be applied in practice, have now been considered by the Higher Courts. The most important decision in the area remains the decision of Julian Knowles J in *London Organising Committee of the Olympic & Paralympic Games (in Liquidation) v Haydn Sinfield* [2018] EWHC 51 (QB), which warrants a detailed consideration.

Facts and First Instance Judgment

Mr Sinfiled volunteered to assist at the 2012 London Olympics and, on the 9th September 2012, he was injured whilst doing so. He fell on his left arm, breaking the left distal radius and the ulnar styloid of his left wrist. The injury had some long-term consequences in relation to what he could and could not do. The Claimant presented a Schedule of loss, verified in the ordinary way with a Statement of Truth. The Schedule included a claim in respect of both past and future gardening services. The Claimant asserted that before the accident he had looked after the garden himself, with his wife, and that post-accident, his wife continued to do some gardening, but they had had to employ a gardener for 2 – 4 hours per week. The past loss equated to £4,992 plus interest; the future loss claim was pleaded at £8,961.31. The total value of the gardening claim, excluding interest, was therefore £13,953.31. The total value of special damages claimed was £33,340.86, meaning the gardening claim equated to 41.9% of the total special damages claim. Liability was admitted and damages for pain, suffering and loss of amenity were agreed at £16,000. Thus, the gardening claim represented about 28% of the damages claim overall. In support of his past gardening loss claim the Claimant disclosed a number of "invoices" from a Mr Mervyn Price, and a Mr Dan Hardy, both said to be gardeners.

The Claimant served an updated Schedule of Loss and maintained, with minor adjustments due to dates, the claims for past and future gardening services. The sum then claimed was £14,785.31, exclusive of interest. The Claimant supported the gardening claim in his witness statement and stated that, "*Pre-accident Christine* [his wife] *and I did all the gardening…*"

The Defendant approached Mr Price, who gave evidence at trial, and confirmed that (i) he had worked for the Claimant and his wife since May 2005 (i.e. pre-accident); (ii) the invoices the Claimant had produced had not been issued by him; and (iii) he had worked for the Claimant between May 2005 and March 2014, when he retired, and the level of his work had not changed after the Claimant's accident.

In light of Mr Price's evidence, the Defendant amended its Defence to plead a case of fundamental dishonesty, and relied on s. 57 of the 2015 Act. The Defendant asserted that the alleged dishonesty was: (i) the assertions in the Schedules of Loss; (ii) the provision of invoices created by the Claimant to support a dishonest claim for expenditure on commercial gardening assistance; and (iii) the Claimant's assertion in his witness statement that by reason of the accident he had been required to employ a gardener to do gardening which he had previously done in conjunction with his wife.

The Claimant served a supplementary witness statement in which he agreed that: Mr Price had been employed by him since 2005; his first witness statement was wrong and had been worded badly, however he and his wife had done a lot of the gardening themselves but after the accident he had been unable to do so; and admitted to preparing the invoices himself. The Claimant served a further Schedule of Damages, reducing the level of his gardening claim to £1,657.96, inclusive of interest.

At first instance, the Recorder held that the Claimant was muddled, confused and careless about the gardening claim but that there was insufficient evidence from which it could be inferred the Claimant had been dishonest about it. The Judge did conclude that the Claimant had not indicated that the invoices which were produced had been created by him on a "self-billing" basis (i.e. producing his own invoices for the work Mr Price had done), and the Judge rejected the Claimant's assertion that he was entitled to "self-bill". The Judge noted that the Claimant had laid himself open to the obvious suggestion that the production of the invoices was an inherently dishonesty action. The Judge indicated that the only conclusion he could draw about the invoices was that they, "*were prepared to pursue the claim, which had been started in this muddled and careless fashion*". He considered that that motivation was of relevance to some extent and he found that,

> "*...part of Mr Sinfield's motivation was to conceal the earlier muddle in which he found himself at this time. The schedule of loss then followed, which repeated the earlier errors, and by this time, Mr Sinfield had put himself in an impossible position. By presenting his claim carelessly and inaccurately in providing invoices without disclosing that they were created by him, his position was extremely difficult.*"

The Recorder held that the Claimant's assertion in his first witness statement, as to the gardening situation, was also dishonest.

Decision of the High Court

Julian Knowles J concluded that the Judge had found, at least by the time the Claimant had made his list of documents and his first witness statement (in August 2016 and October 2016, respectively), that the

Claimant was knowingly making false statements in pursuit of his claim and that he was, by then, acting with a dishonest state of mind in order to justify what had been said in the preliminary schedule of loss.

Julian Knowles J also observed that the Recorder had found that the dishonesty was fundamental to the gardening claim, but that it did not "*contaminate the entire claim*". His Lordship observed that the Recorder had concluded that the Claimant had made a "*careless error in the initial presentation of part of his case, which he later compounded by attempting to conceal it. The dishonesty was motivated not by a wish to create a false claim, but to conceal and get away with the muddled and careless presentation of this case in the past*". The Recorder's judgment showed that he had considered the dishonesty went solely to the gardening claim; the Claimant had a genuine claim for damages for gardening losses but failed to present it in a proper manner; and the Claimant thereby created an exaggeration of that part of the claim, but it was peripheral to the main claim. Moreover, his Lordship observed that the Recorder had concluded that the Claimant was not fundamentally dishonesty but that even if he were wrong about that, it would be substantially unjust for the entire claim to be dismissed when the dishonesty related to a peripheral part of the claim.

Julian Knowles J considered the meaning of '*fundamental dishonesty*' as in the cases of *Howlett*, and *Gosling*. He also considered (at [57 – 59]) a number of County Court decisions in relation to the application of that concept in the context of CPR r. 44.16(1).

His Lordship then provided the leading guidance on the application of s. 57. At [62] – [63] he stated (emphasis supplied):

> 62. "*In my judgment, a claimant should be found to be fundamentally dishonest within the meaning of s 57(1)(b) if the defendant proves on a balance of probabilities that the claimant has acted dishonestly in relation to the primary claim and/or a related claim (as defined in s 57(8)),* ***and that he has thus substantially affected the***

presentation of his case, either in respects of liability or quantum, in a way which potentially adversely affected the defendant in a significant way, judged in the context of the particular facts and circumstances of the litigation. *Dishonesty is to be judged according to the test set out by the Supreme Court in Ivey v Genting Casinos Limited (t/a Crockfords Club), supra.*

63. ***By using the formulation 'substantially affects' I am intending to convey the same idea as the expressions 'going to the root' or 'going to the heart' of the claim. By potentially affecting the defendant's liability in a significant way 'in the context of the particular facts and circumstances of the litigation' I mean (for example) that a dishonest claim for special damages of £9000 in a claim worth £10 000 in its entirety should be judged to significantly affect the defendant's interests, notwithstanding that the defendant may be a multi-billion pound insurer to whom £9000 is a trivial sum."***

It is certainly arguable on the basis of the dicta in paragraph 63 of the judgment in *LOCOG*, that there is a harmonisation as between the meaning of 'fundamental dishonesty' as it relates to QOCS, and the meaning of 'fundamental dishonesty' as it relates to s. 57 of the 2015 Act.

His Lordship then set out the approach to be adopted by Judges when considering an application under s. 57 for the claim's dismissal. At [64] he stated:

"Where an application is made by a defendant for the dismissal of a claim under s 57 the court should:

(a) *Firstly, consider whether the claimant is entitled to damages in respect of the claim. If he concludes that the claimant is not so entitled, that is the end of the matter, although the judge may have to go on to consider whether to disapply QOCS pursuant to CPR r 44.16.*

(b) *If the judge concludes that the claimant is entitled to damages, the judge must determine whether the defendant has proved to the civil standard that the claimant has been fundamentally dishonest in relation to the primary claim and/or a related claim in the sense that I have explained;*

(c) *If the judge is so satisfied then the judge must dismiss the claim including, by virtue of s 57(3), any element of the primary claim in respect of which the claimant has not been dishonest unless, in accordance with s 57(2), the judge is satisfied that the claimant would suffer substantial injustice if the claim were dismissed."*

In determining the appeal, Julian Knowles J concluded that:

(a) The only reasonable meaning which could be ascribed to the Claimant's assertions contained in his Schedules of Loss was that at the date of the accident it was solely he and his wife who tended the garden and no-one else and that, post-accident, for the first time, he had been required to engage a gardener. That state of affairs was not true and obviously known by the Claimant to be untrue. The Recorder was plainly wrong not to have reached the conclusion that the content of the Schedules of Loss were dishonest misstatements by the Claimant, so as to generate the recoverable losses which he set out.

(b) Even on the basis of the undisturbed findings which the Recorder did make, he was wrong in not concluding, on the balance of probabilities, that the Claimant had been fundamentally dishonest in relation to the claim. The Claimant had presented a claim for special damages in a significant sum, which was evidenced by the dishonest creation of false invoices and by a dishonest witness statement. Both those acts of dishonesty were premeditated and maintained over many months, until the Defendant's solicitors uncovered the true picture. The Claimant had presented his case on quantum in a dishonest way which could have resulted in the Defendant paying out far more than they could properly, on honest evidence, have been ordered to do following a trial.

(c) If the Claimant has been 'fundamentally dishonest' in the way indicated, the fact that the greater part of the claim might be honest is neither here nor there (subject to "substantial injustice"). s. 57(3) required that the entire claim, including any genuine parts, should be dismissed.

(d) There were no findings capable of substantiating a conclusion that there would be "substantial injustice" if the claim were dismissed.

Accordingly, the appeal was allowed and the entire claim was dismissed.

CHAPTER EIGHTEEN SOME OTHER RELEVANT AUTHORITIES

There have been a number of other relevant authorities concerning the issue of 'fundamental dishonesty' and the application of s. 57, of which practitioners should be aware.

(a) Mirajuddin Molodi v (1) Cambridge Vibration Maintenance Service; (2) Aviva Insurance Limited [2018] EWHC 1288 (QB)

Molodi concerned a road traffic accident on the 4th February 2015 as a result of which the Claimant alleged to have sustained injuries to his right hand, right shoulder and neck, and his upper and middle back. The Claimant also brought claims for physiotherapy charges (£1,160) and the cost of repairing his vehicle (£1,293). The Claimant asserted that he had not yet incurred the costs of repairs because he did not "*... understand why I should repair something out of my own pocket when the accident was not my fault*". The Defendant admitted that the collision was caused as a result of their insured's negligence, but argued that it was of such minor severity that it was incapable of causing, or alternatively as a matter of fact did not cause, the Claimant to suffer any injury whatsoever. It was what might be considered a 'classic low velocity causation defence'.

At trial, the Defendants led evidence from the driver and his passenger, that the collision was very minor. The Claimant's evidence, written and oral, was littered with inconsistency, contradiction, and demonstrable untruths (see the discussion at [17 – 21] and [23 – 26]). Nevertheless, notwithstanding those issues with the Claimant's case, at first instance HHJ Main Q.C. considered it was more likely than not that the Claimant had suffered some relatively short-term injury and accordingly entered judgment in his favour for damages in the sum of £4,397.

The Defendant appealed and argued that the trial Judge had failed to pay sufficient regard to the inconsistencies and contradictions in the Claimant's evidence and pleaded case, together with his propensity for exaggeration. The Defendant relied on the following matters:

- The claimant had advanced a claim for £1,300 for the cost of repairs to his damaged vehicle on the basis that such repairs had not yet been carried out but, as had been established in cross-examination, had actually already had it repaired by a friend for about £400;

- There was a contradiction between the CNF and the Claimant's evidence as to whether the Claimant was the only occupant of the vehicle or whether he had a male passenger with him;

- The CNF also said that the Claimant had no rehabilitation needs when the Claimant had then made a claim for 12 sessions of physiotherapy;

- The Claimant asserted in his evidence that he had taken time off work but the CNF stated there was no time off work. Moreover, he had not made a claim for lost earnings notwithstanding the fact that in his witness statement he asserted that due to the accident had been unable to work his normal hours for about two weeks and for three days post-accident had not worked at all;

- The Claimant told his expert that he had only been involved in one previous accident. He repeated that assertion in his witness statement. In fact, he had been involved in at least four previous accidents, and probably more, possibly as many as seven (on appeal Counsel for the Claimant accepted that there had been five, perhaps six, previous accidents).

The Defendant argued that those matters should have led HHJ Main Q.C. to make a finding of fundamental dishonesty against the Claimant and to have dismissed the claim pursuant to s. 57 of the 2015 Act. The High Court allowed the appeal, holding that the claim should be dismissed pursuant to s. 57 on the basis of the Claimant's fundamental dishonesty [in fact, Martin Spencer J went further, holding that HHJ Main Q.C. should have dismissed the claim because the Claimant had failed to prove his case].

Molodi is important for two primary reasons:

(a) First, at paragraph 48 of the judgment, Martin Spencer J adopts, and thus endorses, the test to be applied when considering an application under s. 57, as expounded by Julian Knowles J in *LOCOG*.

(b) Secondly, because Martin Spencer J gives general and important guidance to first instance Judges as to how they should approach the assessment of claims involving alleged whiplash injuries, particularly in the context of considerations of 'fundamental dishonesty'. The now well-known (and oft quoted) passages of his Lordship's dicta are worth setting out, in full:

> 43. *"Before considering the particular issues in this case, it is also pertinent to recognise the problem that fraudulent or exaggerated whiplash claims have presented for the insurance industry and the courts. This was recognised in March 2018 when the Ministry of Justice published a Civil Liability Bill which aims to tackle insurance fraud in the UK through tougher measures on fraudulent whiplash claims, proposing new, fixed caps on claims and banning the practise of seeking or offering to settle whiplash claims without medical evidence. The problem of fraudulent and exaggerated whiplash claims is well recognised and should, in my judgment, cause judges in the County Court to*

approach such claims with a degree of caution, if not suspicion. Of course, where a vehicle is shunted from the rear at a sufficient speed to cause the heads of those in the motorcar to move forwards and backwards in such a way as to be liable to cause "whiplash" injury, then genuine claimants should recover for genuine injuries sustained. The court would normally expect such claimants to have sought medical assistance from their GP or by attending A & E, to have returned in the event of non-recovery, to have sought appropriate treatment in the form of physiotherapy (without the prompting or intervention of solicitors) and to have given relatively consistent accounts of their injuries, the progression of symptoms and the timescale of recovery when questioned about it for the purposes of litigation, whether to their own solicitors or to an examining medical expert or for the purposes of witness statements. Of course, I recognise that claimants will sometimes make errors or forget relevant matters and that 100% consistency and recall cannot reasonably be expected. However, the courts are entitled to expect a measure of consistency and certainly, in any case where a claimant can be demonstrated to have been untruthful or where a claimant's account has been so hopelessly inconsistent or contradictory or demonstrably untrue that their evidence cannot be promoted as having been reliable, the court should be reluctant to accept that the claim is genuine or, at least, deserving of an award of damages.

[...]

45. *In the present case, in my judgment, HHJ Main QC adopted a much too benevolent approach to evidence from a claimant which could be demonstrated to be inconsistent, unreliable and, on occasions, simply untruthful. The most glaring example of this relates to Mr Molodi's clear lie to*

Dr Idoko, confirmed by Dr Idoko in his Part 35 answers, that he had been involved in only one previous accident when, as conceded by Mr Sweeney, there had been five or six previous accidents or, on Mr Wood's submissions, some seven previous accidents. Not only had the Claimant lied to Dr Idoko in this regard, but he had also maintained that lie in his witness statement, endorsed with a statement of truth. Even when he gave evidence before HHJ Main QC, the Claimant confirmed that he was happy to rely on the contents of Dr Idoko's report even though he must have known that it was wrong in a fundamental respect.

46. *The medical evidence is at the heart of claims for whiplash injuries. Given the proliferation of claims that are either dishonest or exaggerated, for a medical report to be reliable, it is essential that the history given to the medical expert is as accurate as possible. This includes the history in relation to previous accidents as this goes to fundamental questions of causation: whether, if there are ongoing symptoms, those are attributable to the index accident or to previous accidents or to some idiopathic condition of the claimant. Furthermore, the knowledge that a claimant has been involved in many previous accidents might cause a medical expert to look rather more closely at what is being alleged on the incident occasion to see whether the claimant is being consistent and whether his reported injuries are in accordance with the reported circumstances of the accident. Once, as here, the Claimant could be shown to have been dishonest in respect of a fundamental matter and then to have maintained that dishonesty through his witness statement and into his evidence before the Court, it is difficult to see how the Learned Judge could have accepted any other part of the Claimant's evidence or the medical report itself – and, without these, there was nothing left.*

> 47. *However, the Claimant's dishonesty did not stop there: Mr Wood demonstrated clearly that £1,300 special damages were claimed in respect of a loss which, when investigated in cross-examination, turned out to have been only been £400. There were fundamental inconsistencies between what the Claimant was saying in his witness statement and evidence, and what he had said in the Claim Notification Form. There were inconsistencies in relation to the period before recovery from the injuries. Finally, it appeared that the Claimant had undergone a course of physiotherapy more for reasons to do with his claim rather than for genuine medical reasons."*

(b) Susan Richards (2) Zane McGrann v Edna Morris [2018] EWHC 1289 (QB)

In *Richards*, Martin Spencer J was again asked to overturn a first instance decision of HHJ Main Q.C.

The Claimants were involved in a road traffic accident on the 18th July 2014. The First Claimant was the driver; the Second Claimant was a front passenger. Liability for the accident was never in dispute. The Defendant disputed the Claimants claims on the basis that this was a very low speed impact which was incapable of causing injury and had, as a matter of fact, not caused injury.

Following the trial, HHJ Main Q.C. entered judgment for both claimants, awarding them each £2,500 for general damages, but dismissing both their special damages claims – the First Claimant had claimed for the pre-accident value of her 'written off' vehicle as well as physiotherapy treatment; the Second Claimant claimed for the cost of a physiotherapy assessment (but no treatment, none having been undertaken).

On appeal, the Defendant argued that the trial Judge should have found the claims to have been dishonest. Ultimately, Martin Spencer J found that the evidence at trial led to an unanswerable case presented by the Defendant that the Claimants had failed to prove their cases. In finding for the Claimants, HHJ Main Q.C. had adopted a "*much too benevolent approach to evidence from Claimants which could be demonstrated to be inconsistent, unreliable and, on occasions, downright untruthful*" (at [66]). However, Martin Spencer J declined to make a finding of fundamental dishonesty on the basis he had not seen or heard the Claimants for himself, nor had an opportunity to assess them as witnesses.

In the context of 'fundamental dishonesty' *Richards* is important for two reasons:

(a) First, Martin Spencer J used the judgment as another opportunity to highlight what he again called the "*...problem that fraudulent or exaggerated whiplash claims have presented for the insurance industry and the court*" (at [65]). He quoted, verbatim, paragraph 44 of his earlier judgment in *Molodi*.

(b) Secondly, the learned Judge stressed the importance of Claims Notification Forms. He did so against the backdrop of the Defendant's numerous and forceful submissions on appeal in relation to inconsistencies as between the content of the CNFs and the other evidence in the case. Adopting a polar opposite approach to HHJ Main Q.C., his Lordship stated (at [7 – 9]):

> *"7. I interpose to make two comments about CNFs generally. Firstly, CNFs are important documents because not only are they the first notification of a claim to the potential defendant's insurer in low value personal injury claims in road traffic accidents where the damages sought are between £1,000 - £25,000 but also they will often be the basis for early settlement of the*

claim. Thus, a claim may go no further than the submission of a CNF and an offer of settlement based on it, which is accepted.

8. Secondly, and linked to the first point, the statement of truth is thus important as it means, or should mean, that the insurer can rely on the accuracy of the contents of the CNF in assessing the damages and any offer of compensation to be made. Where the statement of truth is signed by a claims manager on the claimants' behalf, as here, the insurer trusts the claims manager and, through him or her, the firm of solicitors to have taken proper instructions and to have verified the accuracy of the contents of the document. It is worth remembering the provisions of the practice direction to Part 22 of the Civil Procedure Rules which states:

> *"3.8 Where a legal representative has signed a statement of truth, his signature will be taken by the court as a statement –*
>
> > *1) that the client on whose behalf he has signed and has authorised him to do so*
> >
> > *2) that before signing he had explained to the client that in signing the statement of truth he would be confirming the client's belief that the facts stated in the document are true*
> >
> > *3) that before signing he had informed the client of the possible consequences to the client if it should subsequently appear that the client did not have an honest belief in the truth of those facts."*

CPR 32.14, relating to false statements, provides that "proceedings for contempt of court may be brought against a person if he makes, or causes to be made, a false statement in a doc-

ument verified by a statement of truth without an honest belief in its truth."

9. For the above reasons, I cannot associate myself with the comment made by HHJ Main QC at paragraph 42 of his judgment where, referring to CNFs, he said:

> *"I do not find them reliable documents. They are done shortly. They are all very summarised. They are simplistic documents which do not permit there to be details of clinical presentation that can be relied upon by a trial judge and I just ignore them."*

On the contrary, in my view they are important documents: they provide the basis for possible proceedings for contempt of court, as seen, and they provide valuable information at an early stage in the litigation process. Endorsed with a statement of truth, as they are, CNFs should be reliable documents and should be taken seriously."

(c) *Edward Wright v Satellite Information Services Limited* [2018] EWHC 812 (QB)

In *Wright* the claim arose out of an accident at work on the 24th January 2014 when the Claimant suffered injuries affecting his right lower limb, including a comminuted intra-articular tibial fracture, meaning he was unable to return to work post-accident. The Defendant admitted liability but quantum remained in issue. At trial, the Defendant argued that the claim should be dismissed pursuant to s. 57 of the 2015 Act on the basis that covert video surveillance it had obtained evidenced that the Claimant was far less disabled than he claimed to be and that he had deliberately and dishonestly exaggerated him claim.

The matter came on for trial before HHJ Pearce. The Judge identified some "*real inconsistencies*" in the Claimant's case, including how far he was able to walk; how much he needed to use a walking stick; and the level of pain he suffered. He also considered that there were features of the presentation of the case giving rise to the suggestion that the claim was overstated. In support of its submission that the Claimant was fundamentally dishonest, the Defendant relied heavily on the claim for care which had been advanced, including a future care claim of £73,000. The Judge, having considered the care claim held that, "*given the low levels of care to which the Claimant referred to in his evidence, it is difficult to see that assistance at the levels described by Ms O'Brien* [his care expert] *and adopted as part of the Claimant's case [in] the updated schedule of loss at 1/127 can be justified*".

In the course of giving his judgment, the Judge expressed his concern that the figures set out in Ms O'Brien's report significantly overstated the care that the Claimant required, which the Claimant himself had readily acknowledged. He described the care expert's report as "*fundamentally unreliable*".

Ultimately, HHJ Pearce awarded the Claimant just £2,100 to cover the provision of some future care following future surgery and he took the view that there was no true continuing care need. He also found that the Claimant had not been dishonest, still less fundamentally so, and awarded the Claimant £119,165.02 in damages.

On appeal the Defendant contended that the claim ought to have been dismissed pursuant to s.57 of the 2015 Act on the basis that the Claimant had been fundamentally dishonest. It did so relying on the fact that, having found that the claim for the cost of care was not established, HHJ Pearce was wrong as a matter of law not to find that the Clamant had been dishonest in his presentation of that element of the claim and that such dishonesty was 'fundamental'. The trial Judge's findings of fact were not challenged on appeal. The Defendant argued that the dishonesty lay in presenting a claim for care with reference to the expert's report when the Claimant must have known he did not have such a claim.

Yip J had no hesitation in dismissing the appeal. She carefully considered how the Claimant had actually presented his claim for care at trial, by revisiting the content of his witness statements, the care report itself, and the various Schedules of Loss. She noted that after his first witness statement the Claimant, "*...did not labour the point as far as his care claim was concerned in his further statements*" (at [25]). She observed that the Claimant had, in fact, been broadly consistent in what he had said in relation to a need for ongoing assistance. The rejection of his claim for care had been as a result of a proper analysis, by HHJ Pearce, as to what was actually being done for the Claimant and the conclusion that this did not properly sound in damages (at [31]). A proper reading of HHJ Pearce's decision showed that the rejection of the care claim was due to the fact that a proper interpretation of the evidence did not support the assessment of the care expert; not that the Claimant's evidence had been untruthful. Yip J observed that it would have been surprising if the trial Judge had found the rejection of the bulk of the future car claim in itself, when set in context, did support a finding of dishonesty.

The decision in *Wright* propounds no new statement of principle, it is simply an incidence of the application of the previously understood approach to s. 57. It is, however, a helpful and useful reminder that the mere advancing of a particular head of loss, at a particular level (perhaps a surprisingly high one) which is ultimately rejected at trial does not, in and of itself, equate to dishonesty sufficient to activate s. 57. The *reasons* that the particular claim fails, or is vastly reduced, are all important. In *Wright*, the reason for the extreme reduction was not that the Claimant had dishonestly inflated the sum claimed, but rather problems with the expert evidence and a conclusion that the services claimed for, about which the Claimant had been consistent in his evidence, did not sound in damages. Naturally, each case will turn on its own facts.

(d) David Pinkus v Direct Line [2018] EWHC Civ 1671 (QB)

In *Pinkus* the Claimant was involved in a road traffic accident on the 21st August 2012. Liability was admitted in full. The Claimant's case was that he had suffered significant psychological/psychiatric injuries, as well as minor physical injuries. He claimed to have suffered PTSD and dissociative symptoms. He claimed that he had lost his job just a few weeks post-accident due to the accident's effects on his performance. He had not worked to any meaningful extent (save a few largely unsuccessful attempts at short-term decorating) since the accident. He claimed his family life had been affected, and his symptoms had deteriorated over time. His claim for special damages was in the region of £850,000 and comprised past loss of earnings of £231,930; future loss of earnings of £498,490; and a claim for care in the sum of £46,706. It was said that general damages for pain, suffering and loss of amenity were worth £55,000.

In sharp contrast, the Defendant argued that the Claimant sustained some minor physical injury in the accident and some short-lived travel anxiety/adjustment disorder which resolved by early 2013. The disputed that the accident was of such severity as to cause PTSD. They argued that the claim was exaggerated or fabricated and it was worth no more than £2,000 - £3,000 and that the Claimant had been 'fundamentally' dishonest.

An interesting preliminary point arose (see [5] – [16]) in relation to whether or not the Defendant ought to be permitted to advance a case of 'fundamental dishonesty' at trial on the basis that such a pleading was made late (it was only on the first day of trial that a Counter Schedule of Loss was signed directly pleading 'fundamental dishonesty') and inadequately, inter alia, because the Defendant made reference to matters "*to be explored in cross-examination*" and used the phrase "*for example*". It was argued that the Defence made it clear there would be other matters which the Defendant clearly intended to rely upon which had not been detailed and therefore the pleading was defective. HHJ

Coe Q.C. (sitting as a High Court Judge) applied the same principles as espoused by Newey LJ in *Howlett* to hold that the Defendant was permitted to run such an argument – it had been clear to the Claimant from the outset of the litigation and throughout that the Defendant denied the accident had occurred as the Claimant alleged; the Defence had put causation and quantum in issue; the Defendant had used surveillance which made it apparent the Claimant's credibility was in issue; the Claimant knew there were issues with the medical evidence which made conscious exaggeration at least a possibility; the Claimant knew of the Defendant's valuation of the claim; and by the time of the trial, he knew the detail of the matters in the Counter Schedule which made specific allegations of conscious and gross exaggeration. In short, the Claimant had, as the Judge put it, had "*known "what he was facing" for some time*" (at [12]).

The decision in *Pinkus* therefore supports the contention that the manner in which a Defendant should prepare/advance its case on 'fundamental dishonesty' does not differ as between the application of s. 57 of the 2015 Act and the application of CPR r. 44.16(1) – the guidance in *Howlett* should be followed in both circumstances.

After a lengthy trial, HHJ Coe Q.C. awarded the Claimant just £4,250 for general damages, and £250 for his policy excess. The judgment made numerous significant findings against the Claimant, including:

(a) In relation to the accident itself, the Claimant alleged he had been travelling at 70mph when the Defendant's driver's vehicle hit him at close to 100mph. He considered he was about to suffer a fatal injury. He claimed he had been subject to violent deceleration and rotational forces. Although he said in oral evidence, he had not struck the central reservation his updated Schedule of Loss claimed that he had been pushed into it. Some of the documents also suggested he had told a treating physician that he had hit the crash barrier. The Judge found that the Claimant had deliberately given the impression he collided with a crash barrier on the M4. He had been untruthful in describing the collision and had consciously exaggerated the trauma of the incident. The accident had not involved rotational forces or violent deceleration;

(b) The Claimant had been deliberately obstructive in failing to identify a counsellor who had been engaged pre-accident to deal with his teenage son's behavioural issues. The Court rejected the Claimant's case about the extent of the difficulties experienced with his son pre-collision; they were more significant than the Claimant was prepared to accept and he had deliberately minimised them;

(c) The Claimant implied that post-accident he did not drive to work, past the accident site, or on motorways. The Judge found that he had driven to work on the motorway post-accident and his suggestion otherwise was reflective of his exaggeration of the accident and its impact on him;

(d) Pre-accident, the Claimant worked in the film industry as an assistant director; he had been reasonably successful. The Claimant's case was that after the accident he became temperamentally so volatile that he was unable to function effectively at work; he had become argumentative with his colleagues and generally disruptive. He claimed that he had lost his temper and accordingly been fired. He alleged that he had refused work offers because he was struggling with emotional issues and would have been perceived as weak and would have been stigmatised as having emotional problems. The Judge found that the Claimant had failed to establish, on balance, that he had been fired due to his volatility. Offers of further work, post-accident, which the Claimant had rejected, did not support the suggestion that there were issues with his work in the film industry. He had been dishonest in suggesting he had been fired because of a row with his immediate boss in consequence of his loss of anger control. He had chosen not to return to that work due to a combination of family issues, his wife's new business and difficulties with his son's behaviour. His failure to return to work was not due to any sequalae of the accident;

(e) The Claimant said he had poor financial skills, not being able to add up the price of coffee and cake, but that was rejected – the Claimant had negotiated a deal to carry out a building renovation job post-accident and had been persistently difficult about the division of the final payment at the conclusion of the job;

(f) The Claimant had asserted he could not withstand banter; yet the Court found he had been heavily involved in such conduct at decorating jobs he had carried out post-accident, including winding people up and playing practical jokes;

(g) On one renovation job, the Claimant had told those around him that he was affected by the noise of the nail gun due to his PTSD. The Court considered that was significant as it was said at a time when the Claimant had begun reporting PTSD symptoms. HHJ Coe Q.C. found it to be part of the Claimant's fabrication of his symptoms;

(h) The Claimant had asserted that he had not told his wife or son about his PTSD and the significant issues with which he was suffering for some considerable time post-accident. HHJ Coe Q.C. found that to be a lie. Such an assertion was inconsistent with the account in both the Claimant's and his wife's witness statements as to the reasons for a fishing trip that the Claimant went on to America. Secondly, it was inconsistent with one of the Claimant's treating practitioner's contemporaneous notes that the Claimant's wife was not being sympathetic about his condition. Thirdly, both the Claimant's wife and his son would have noticed the changes in behaviour and serious deterioration alleged, had the Claimant actually been displaying those sorts of behaviours and suffering in the ways asserted;

(i) Facebook evidence showed that the Claimant continued to post regularly; have a large circle of friends; travel abroad; engage in political and current issues and debates; and continue to be involved in discussions about the film industry. They gave the impression that the Claimant had a happy family and he was enjoying everyday activities and sharing them;

(j) He had given inconsistent accounts about his psychiatric injuries and their impacts on him to various practitioners (treating and expert) following the accident;

(k) The Claimant's reporting of symptoms of PTSD was fabricated and reported dishonestly;

(l) The Claimant had failed the effort tests administered by the Defendant's neuropsychologist; this had been because he had deliberately feigned slowness but was insufficiently expert to achieve consistency. Having decided to deliberately take too long to carry out the first part of the colour word interference test, he deliberately took too long to carry out the second part, which was harder, failing to appreciate that he was in fact demonstrating better effort at the harder tests. Failing the tests was a reflection of his fabrication and/or exaggeration;

(m) He had deliberately lied about his ability to follow a newspaper or book. The Judge found that throughout the relevant period, he had been able to read long articles and absorb, process and retain the information and comment on it. The Judge could "*well understand*" how the man in the witness box might not be able to read an article, but it was not consistent with his activities as evidenced by some of the Facebook posts, or the debates he entered into (specifically in relation to the United Kingdom's referendum on whether or not to leave the European Union) whilst on the decorating jobs;

(n) He had exaggerated or deliberately fabricated an impairment of taste and tinnitus, or falsely sought to attribute them to the accident;

(o) The Claimant's wife described him in her evidence as being dirty, unwashed and unkempt; she said he hardly ever bothered to shave and described his appearance as "*disgusting*". HHJ Coe Q.C. considered that some aspects of his presentation were deliberately staged, for example he attended the second day of his evidence clearly not having shaved which the Judge considered to be a "*deliberate ploy*";

(p) The Claimant had deliberately exaggerated and fabricated symptoms in Court, which he did not display in real life. He had consciously exaggerated his symptoms;

(q) His performance in the witness box was unconvincing. The Judge considered it was notable that his memory apparently failed him when he was being asked more challenging questions about his credibility but it was clear when he wished to make a point about the extent of his difficulties. He had displayed extreme forgetfulness and confusion throughout his evidence but when he wanted to emphasise a point in favour of his case, or deny a point being made against him, he could be clear, articulate, and direct.

The Court was invited to dismiss the claim, in its entirety, pursuant to s. 57 of the 2015 Act. Unsurprisingly, that application was granted. The Court considered that the Claimant had not been honest in many respects; had deliberately exaggerated his symptoms to both experts and treating doctors; had fabricated many symptoms; had been dishonest about his pre-accident circumstance; and had been dishonest about his post-accident functioning. His exaggeration and fabrication was intentional with the purpose of inflating his claim. The fabrication was "*extreme*". Additionally, he had exaggerated the nature and severity of the collision itself. The Court also confirmed that, in line with *Aviva v*

Kovacic [2017] EWHC 2772 (QB) it was satisfied to the criminal standard of proof in respect of the findings of deliberate exaggeration and dishonesty.

The Court was not satisfied that the Claimant would suffer any 'substantial injustice' if the claim were dismissed; the obvious reason for the Claimant's fabrication was financial game; the Judge could think of no other reason why the Claimant would behave as he had.

Beyond confirming that the guidance in *Howlett* applies equally in relation to the manner in which a case of 'fundamental dishonesty' should be run in the context of s. 57 of the 2015 Act, *Pinkus* propounds no new statement of principle. It is another example of the application of s. 57 to the facts of a particular case. It is interesting that in *Pinkus* there was no single 'silver bullet' (as there was in *Gosling* and *Patel* – both cases turning, essentially, on the content of the Defendant's covert surveillance). In large part, the Claimant's undoing in *Pinkus* was as a result of a most forensic consideration and analysis of his reporting and presenting history from the date of the accident onwards and its inconsistency with other contemporaneous evidence; and his extremely poor performance in the witness box.

(e) Jason Roberts v (1) Alan Kesson; (2) Tesco Underwriting Limited [2020] EWHC 521 (QB).

In *Roberts* the claim concerned a road traffic accident in July 2017. The Second Defendant was suspicious about the circumstances of the accident but, at first instance, Recorder Kelbrick found that the accident was the result of the negligent driving of the First Defendant. At the time of the accident the Claimant was driving a Mercedes E250 which suffered significant damage all along its' nearside. The Claimant's Schedule of Loss, supported by a Statement of Truth, claimed the pre-accident value of the vehicle in the sum of £10,400, on the basis that the vehicle was, in effect, a 'write off'.

In his first witness statement, dated the 6th March 2018, the Claimant confirmed that the engineer's report advised the vehicle was to be written off and stated that he had authorised the sale of his vehicle for salvage, which salvage monies he then used to hire a replacement taxi on a cash basis. He maintained his claim for the pre-accident value of £10,400. The Second Defendant undertook enquiries which revealed that on the 5th March 2018 (i.e. the day before the Claimant signed his first witness statement) the Claimant's Mercedes had passed its MOT. They also discovered Facebook entries in which the Claimant was seeking to sell the vehicle in a roadworthy state, backed by the MOT certificate, for £7,000.

Having had those enquiries brought to his attention, the Claimant produced a second witness statement in which he said that, on reflection, the first statement was accurate, "*save for one small detail*". On appeal, the High Court subsequently remarked that the second statement did not fully explain the true picture in respect of vehicle disposal, hire charges and what happened thereafter. In his second statement, the Claimant gave evidence that he had sold the vehicle to his brother in law, who ran an auto company, but that his brother in law became frustrated because of delays and, in order to avoid tension between them, in September 2017 the brother in law persuaded the Claimant to take the damaged car back. The Claimant's position then being that in September 2017 the car was returned to him, but in its damaged state. On his own evidence, the Claimant then, apparently, purchased parts for the vehicle, engaged his brother in law to undertake the repairs (which took about a week), following which the car was returned to him.

At trial, it was put to the Claimant that his claim in relation to the £10,400 pre-accident value was dishonest. The Claimant had eventually, and it seems with some reluctance, accepted in oral evidence that his initial witness statement was untrue. The Defendant made submissions on the issue of fundamental dishonesty and, in particular, argued that the entirety of the claim was so infected by dishonesty that s. 57 of the 2015 Act should be activated.

Recorder Kelbrick gave what was described on appeal by Jay J as a "*rather brief*" *ex tempore* judgment. The Recorder did not address specifically the issues joined under s. 57 of the 2015 Act. He addressed the claim for £10,400 and pointed out inconsistencies between the two witness statements. He made a finding that the Claimant had, "*accepted he was dishonest in part when making his first statement, but I do observe that he did not persist with that dishonesty. Whether or not that was because he had been, to use [Counsel for the Defendant's] words – 'flushed out' – or whether it was not, nevertheless he did not persist with it, and did not persist with it in oral cross examination today*". The claim for £10,400 was rejected on the basis there was insufficient evidence to support it. It could have been framed as a claim for the cost of repairs and the diminution in value of the Claimant's Mercedes, but there was no evidence on either of those two matters. The Recorder then dealt with other claims that were before him in relation to storage charges, hire charges and others.

On appeal to the High Court, the Defendant argued that the Recorder's judgment was seriously deficient in relation to the s. 57 issue and that there was a mass of evidence which demonstrated that, in particular, the Claimant's first witness statement was dishonestly untrue. It was argued that the Claimant had stated precisely, and in terms, that the vehicle had been sold when that was not the case, and it was only when the Second Defendant drew attention to that fact, that the Claimant changed his story. The Defendant also relied on the decision of Julian Knowles J in *Haider* in relation to the Claimant's failure to disclose various financial documentation/information in support of a plea of impecuniosity vis-à-vis credit hire charges.

Jay J concluded that the Recorder's reasons for his decision were inadequate; he had not properly addressed the issue of dishonesty. Objectively speaking, Jay J considered that the Claimant's first witness statement was untrue on an important issue (the claim for £10,400 pre-accident value) and the second witness statement did not put the matter right. Jay J considered that the Recorder should have grappled with those matters properly and made clear findings, but he had not done so.

His Lordship was required to then consider whether he could deduce from all the material in the case, what the Recorder's reasons were. If he could not, then he had to decide whether the appeal should be conducted by way of a rehearing, with the High Court determining the issue(s), or whether a retrial would be required.

Jay J observed that that the conducting of a rehearing was not straightforward given a finding of fundamental dishonesty against the Claimant was extremely important and that he should only proceed on that basis if he was "*… driven to conclude that there was only one answer to the fact in issue. If I am in any doubt, I should be going down the separate and different course of directing a new trial.*" (at [48]). In relation to arguments about storage charges, and hire charges, Jay J was not prepared to conclude that there was 'only one answer' such that he should conduct a rehearing (see: [50 – 53]).

However, in relation to the claim for £10,400 pre-accident value, Jay J concluded the result was different – the only permissible conclusion was that the Claimant had been fundamentally dishonest in advancing a false claim in the Schedule of Loss and in his first witness statement. No proper explanation had been given for those falsities and none could possibly exist.

Jay J gave some useful guidance as to the approach to be adopted when considering the operation of s. 57, which is of general application. He said (at [54]) (his Lordship's emphasis maintained):

> "*The language of Section 57 is important. The Court must be satisfied on the balance of probabilities that the Claimant* ***has been*** *fundamentally dishonest. The real question is whether the Claimant*

> *has been fundamentally dishonest and not whether he has persisted in that dishonesty"*

Jay J also considered that the Claimant's dishonesty was 'fundamental'. He adopted the formulation provided by Julian Knowles J in the *LOCOG* case. Jay J also provided further useful, general guidance as to the meaning of 'fundamental' and the approach to be adopted in stating: "*In my view, what is required is a global assessment in light of the claim as advanced in its entirety, but also in view of the saliency and importance of the particular claim under consideration*" (at [60]) and, "*In my judgment, applying that approach, which is necessarily a holistic approach...*" (at [61]).

In a parting comment that is sure to resonate loudly on both sides of personal injury litigation Jay J said (at [61]) (emphasis added):

> "*It was the policy of Parliament in enacting Section 57 that even in circumstances where other claims may be valid, if a party advances a claim which is dishonest and it is significant and substantial,* ***the Court should not be slow to find that the stringent criterion of Section 57 has been fulfilled***".

Roberts is an important decision not least for four reasons:

(a) First, it is a further instance of the High Court endorsing the test to be applied, as set out by Julian Knowles J in the *LOCOG* case;

(b) Secondly, it confirms that what matters for the purpose of applying s. 57 is whether the Claimant *has been* at some stage dishonest, and not whether the Claimant *had been* (or at least *arguably had been*) dishonesty at some prior stage, but had since relented/otherwise not persisted in his/her prior dishonesty;

(c) Thirdly, it reiterates that in considering whether proven dishonesty is 'fundamental' the Court must undertake a global assessment in light of the claim advanced in its entirety *as well as* in view of the saliency and importance of the particular claim under consideration. A "holistic" approach is to be adopted.

(d) Finally, and probably most importantly, it confirms that Courts should not be slow to find that the requirements of s. 57 have been met.

In relation to the final observation made in the immediately preceding paragraph, it is perhaps interesting to note the apparent divergence of views as between the Executive and the Courts, in relation to the readiness with a Judge should find s. 57 is satisfied. Whilst observing that the criteria of s. 57 are "stringent", Jay J's comment that the Court's should "*not be slow to find*" that they have been met does not fit entirely neatly with Lord Faulks Q.C.'s comments in the House of Lords at Committee stage, when he observed, "*I assure the Committee that the way that the clause is drafted should not result in the courts using the measures lightly.*"

CHAPTER NINETEEN
A SECONDARY REQUIREMENT TO SATISFY CPR R. 44.16(1)

In circumstances where the Defendant has successfully persuaded a Court to dismiss the entire claim pursuant to s. 57 of the 2015 Act, that is not the end of the matter. At that stage, the claim will have been dismissed, the Defendant will (presumably) have been awarded its costs of defending the action, but that costs order remains unenforceable by reason of the QOCS provisions. Therefore, after securing dismissal pursuant to s. 57 the Defendant must address the issue of CPR r. 44.16(1) and persuade the Judge that permission should be given to enforce the costs order.

In the overwhelming majority (if not all) cases this final stage in the exercise should not prove problematic. However, it is right to note and be cognisant of an important subtle and technical distinction as between s. 57 and CPR r. 44.16(1) in relation to the source of the dishonesty with which the Court is concerned, when applying the relevant tests. To be clear:

(a) In relation to CPR r. 44.16(1) the dishonesty with which the Court is concerned is that of the **claim**;

(b) In relation to s. 57 of the 2015 Act the dishonesty with which the Court is concerned is that of the **Claimant**, him/herself.

That distinction leaves open the possibility (theoretical at least) that the **Claimant** may have been 'fundamentally dishonest', such that an otherwise compensable claim is dismissed in its entirety pursuant to s. 57 of the 2015 Act, but that the **claim** is not considered to be 'fundamentally dishonesty', and thus the Defendant cannot bring itself within the scope of CPR r. 44.16(1) and thus the costs order made in its favour remains unenforceable.

This issue was expressly identified by Julian Knowles J in *LOCOG* (at [60]) where he said:

> 60. *"Picking up on a point made by the judge in Menary, the drafter of s 57 sought to draw several distinctions from CPR r 44.16: it is the claimant who the court must find dishonest, rather than the claim. Further, rather than permitting the defendant to recover all of his costs, the court is required to assess the claimant's 'genuine' damages and deduct that figure from the defendant's costs. As to the first point, however, it will be rare for a claim to be fundamentally dishonest without the claimant also being fundamentally dishonest, although that might be a theoretical possibility, at least."*

Whilst the theoretical possibility clearly exists as a result of the difference in drafting, it is suggested that, in practice, there is likely to be no case where, having found a Claimant to have been 'fundamentally dishonest' for the purpose of s. 57, a Judge would not also accept that the claim itself was 'fundamentally dishonest' for the purposes of QOCS. It would seem perverse (notwithstanding the technical possibility) that one finding would not follow the other. It also seems unlikely that a Judge will be particularly sympathetic or receptive to such a technical argument made on behalf of the Claimant, given the Court would have just found him/her to be dishonest.

CHAPTER TWENTY
THE MEANING OF "SUBSTANTIAL INJUSTICE"

Having been found to be 'fundamentally dishonest', the Claimant's last roll of the dice in order to avoid losing all the genuine damages to which they would otherwise be entitled, is to attempt to persuade the Court that dismissal of the entire claim would cause him/her to suffer "*substantial injustice*" (s. 57(2)). At the Bill's Committee Stage in the House of Lords, Lord Faulks Q.C. observed that, "*The clause gives the court some flexibility to ensure that the provision is applied fairly and proportionately.*" The decision to enshrine within the primary legislation a mechanism by which the Court may refuse to dismiss the entire claim, it is suggested, is one of public policy, underpinned by an appreciation that the unique facts and circumstances of each case mean that an inflexible approach, which does not facilitate the possibility of any exception being made, is likely to be inappropriate and lead to injustice[1].

The Act itself does not define "*substantial injustice*". A number of decisions of the High Court have touched on the issue but, perhaps conscious that any guidance may unwittingly limit the intended flexibility of the provision, or alternatively impose unwarranted and undesirable parameters on the scope of its application, the Judges have tended to focus more on what "*substantial injustice*" <u>is not</u>, as opposed to what it actually is.

<u>*(a) LOCOG*</u>

In *LOCOG,* Julian Knowles J said, (at [65]) (emphasis added):

---

1 The absence of any provision akin to that provided for in s. 57(2) may also give rise to Human Rights issues.

> *"65. Given the infinite variety of circumstances which might arise, I prefer not to try and be prescriptive as to what sort of facts might satisfy the test of substantial injustice.* ***However, it seems to me plain that substantial injustice must mean more than the mere fact that the claimant will lose his damages for those heads of claim that are not tainted with dishonesty****. That must be so because of s 57(3). Parliament plainly intended that sub-section to be punitive and to operate as a deterrent. It was enacted so that claimants who are tempted to dishonestly exaggerate their claims know that if they do, and they are discovered, the default position is that they will lose their entire damages. It seems to me that it would effectively neuter the effect of s 57(3) if dishonest claimants were able to retain their 'honest' damages by pleading substantial injustice on the basis of the loss of those damages per se. What will generally be required is some substantial injustice arising as a consequence of the loss of those damages."*

(b) *Benius Razumas v Ministry of Justice* [2018] EWHC 215 (QB)

In *Razmus* the Claimant was imprisoned for various periods between 2010 and 2013. The Defendant had overall responsibility for the prisons in which he was incarcerated. It was common ground that, whilst in prison, the medical care the Claimant had received for cancer was deficient in various respects and, as a result of that negligence, he had to have his left leg amputated above the knee. Inter alia, the Claimant claimed damages from the Defendant for personal injury arising from clinical negligence.

The issues before the Judge included whether the Defendant was directly or vicariously liable for the clinical negligence and whether his personal injury claim was barred under s. 57 of the 2015 Act by reason of fundamentally dishonest assertions in his Particulars of Claim. The Claimant had positively asserted in his Particulars of Claim, and had repeated in his evidence, that he had sought medical attention whilst outside prison. The Court found that averment to be was knowingly dishonest. The Claimant had thereby substantially affected the presentation of his case, either in respect of liability or quantum, in a way which potentially adversely affected the Defendant in a significant way. Had the Claimant had a valid claim [it failing on essentially every ground in any event] it would have been dismissed pursuant to s. 57(2).

In *obiter dicta* considering the issue of substantial injustice, Cockerill J observed (at [213] – [215]):

> *213. "I do not consider that there could be any way out for Mr Razumas via the argument on substantial injustice. It cannot in my judgement be right to say that substantial injustice would result in disallowing the claim where a claimant has advanced dishonestly a claim which if established would result in full compensation. That would be to cut across what the section is trying to achieve.*
>
> *214. In the Sinfield case Julian Knowles J had no difficulty in dismissing this argument in the context of a dishonesty which went only to part of the quantum claimed. At [89] he stated that it was plain from section 57(3):*
>
> > *"....something more is required than the mere loss of damages to which the claimant is entitled to establish substantial injustice. Parliament has provided that the default position is that a fundamentally dishonest claimant should lose his damages in their entirety, even though ex hypothesi, by s 57(1), he is properly entitled to some damages. It would render superfluous s 57(3) if the mere loss of genuine damages could constitute substantial injustice."*
>
> *215. This, it seems to me, must be right. Something more is required. That something more is not made out here and so, if there were a claim it would fail at this stage."*

(c) Sudhirkumar Patel v (1) Arriva Midlands Limited; (2) Zurich Insurance PLC [2019] EWHC 1216 (QB)

In *Patel*, HHJ Melissa Clarke (sitting as a Judge of the High Court) said (at [94] – [97]) (emphasis added):

> *"94. The Claimant submits that the court cannot assess substantial injustice without a full quantification of the claim as otherwise it cannot understand the extent of the claim that it is dismissing. I have already set out that I am satisfied that the 'dishonest part' of the claim is the bulk of the pleaded claim by value.*
>
> *95. The Claimant further submits that the court cannot deal with substantial injustice without hearing witness evidence, but is not clear to me that the Claimant has raised any real argument that dismissal of the claim would cause substantial injustice to the Claimant, beyond losing his entitlement to damages for the lesser, 'honest' part of his claim.* ***Mr Hunjan submits orally and in his skeleton argument that Chirag Patel has had to give up his career to look after his father, but I am satisfied this detriment to the son (if detriment there is) cannot in law amount to substantial injustice to the Claimant in the dismissal of the claim.***
>
> ***96. I have mentioned the Claimant's submission that he will require substantial care for the rest of his life, and if the claim is dismissed it will cause substantial injustice as the family do not have the funds to provide for commercial care. However is difficult to understand on what basis that submission is made, given that the only diagnosis is of a conversion disorder which I have found is not tenable. To the extent that the submission is founded on a need for care arising from another diagnosis or potential diagnosis, this is both unpleaded and unevidenced, and so cannot raise issues of substantial injustice arising from dismissal of the pleaded claim, in my judgment.***

> *97. Finally, the Claimant submits that a court cannot without substantial injustice dismiss the claim of the Claimant, a protected party, because of the dishonest conduct of his litigation friend. In my judgment that submission cannot succeed in the circumstances of this case as I have found them to be. Firstly, I have found that the Claimant himself has been fundamentally dishonest in relation to his claim. He has done so by his presentation alone, as well as by not correcting the false impression of the Claimant's disabilities given by his litigation friend to the doctors or his solicitors at any time during the course of these proceedings. Secondly, I have found that the Claimant must be presumed to have capacity in this case."*

Comment on "*substantial injustice*"

Realistically, very little can be gleaned from the cases decided thus far. This is a developing area of the law. At its highest, one might suggest that the following conclusions can be drawn:

(a) The simple fact that, as a result of the dismissal of the claim, the Claimant will lose the "genuine" damages to which he/she would otherwise have been entitled cannot amount to "*substantial injustice*". Something more is required [*LOCOG*; *Razmus v Ministry of Justice*];

(b) There is no inalienable requirement for the Court to hear witness evidence before determining the issue of "*substantial injustice*" [*Patel*];

(c) It would appear that any detriment suffered by a member of the Claimant's family (or arguably any person connected with the Claimant) who would be required to care for the Claimant as a result of the Claimant not recovering damages, cannot amount to "*substantial injustice*". That is to be considered a determinant to the individual, and not the Claimant [*Patel*];

(d) It would appear that the fact a Claimant's family do not have the funds to provide care for him, is unlikely to amount to "*substantial injustice*" [*Patel*].

In reality, having been found to be 'fundamentally dishonesty' it is very difficult to see in what circumstances a Claimant will be 'saved' by successfully arguing that he/she will suffer "*substantial injustice*" if the whole claim is dismissed. The purpose of s. 57 of the 2015 Act is punitive. It is suggested that it will be a truly exceptional case which warrants the application of the "*substantial injustice*" provision. It is difficult to identify or suggest what sort of circumstances may give rise to "*substantial injustice*". It is tentatively suggested that one such situation might be, for example, significant external duress or other threats brought to bear on the Claimant or members of his/her family, resulting in him/her advancing a dishonest claim. Each case is, naturally, highly fact sensitive. No doubt the parameters and application of the provision will continue to be explored in the Courts in the years to come.

CHAPTER TWENTY ONE
THE TIMING OF AN APPLICATION UNDER SECTION 57

When can, or should, an application for a dismissal of the claim pursuant to s. 57 of the 2015 Act be made?

It is not an absolute requirement that both liability **and** quantum have been determined prior to the Court being able to consider, and being able to allow an application for the claim to be dismissed pursuant to s. 57 of the 2015 Act; that was the conclusion of HHJ Clarke in *Sudhirkumar Patel v (1) Arriva Midlands Ltd & (2) Zurich Insurance Plc* [2019] EWHC 1216 (QB).

Sudhirkumar Patel v (1) Arriva Midlands Ltd & (2) Zurich Insurance Plc [2019] EWHC 1216 (QB)

Facts

In *Patel*, the Claimant was a pedestrian who had been struck by the Defendant's bus. Following a trial on liability the Claimant established negligence against the Defendant, subject to a 40% deduction for contributory negligence. At the conclusion of the liability trial, the Defendant made an application to dismiss the claim pursuant to s. 57.

As a result of the accident the Claimant suffered a cardiac arrest and was resuscitated after 4 minutes by a bystander performing CPR. He was conveyed to hospital where he was diagnosed with a subarachnoid haemorrhage and admitted. He was in hospital for a number of weeks before being discharged. The Claimant's case was that despite an initial recovery, he began to deteriorate within a week of the collision and at the time of filing his claim, he was significantly disabled. Neurological experts instructed by both the Claimant and Defendant could find no neurological reason for the Claimant's extreme condition at the time of their respective examinations (with the Claimant found in bed, mute, almost entirely unresponsive, and almost entirely without movement in his body). The Claimant's son, who was also his litigation friend, gave both experts the impression that the Claimant suffered from very severe disability which had been reasonably static; that he said very little and almost nothing he did say was meaningful; that he did nothing for himself; that he required complete care, showing only the slightest participation in personal activities of daily living like washing and toileting; and was largely immobile.

Both experts considered whether the Claimant's condition was feigned. The Claimant's expert ultimately concluded that the condition was not feigned and that he was suffering from a severe conversion disorder. The Defendant's expert felt unable to distinguish between whether the condition was real or feigned. Both experts did, however, agree that the hallmark of a conversion disorder was consistency i.e. unchanging disability regardless of circumstances and whether or not the patient was aware he was being observed.

The Defendant commissioned covert surveillance of the Claimant which showed him in the company of his second son, making a number of visits to seven tyre shops in Leicester over a period of a number of hours, on two separate excursions during the same day. He was seen walking without difficulty; getting into and out of the front passenger seat on multiple occasions unaided and without apparent difficulty; walking around the tyre suppliers, through car parks, and in and out of customer service areas; talking to his son and participating in conversation with various workers at the tyre shops; seemingly interested and engaged in what was happening; reacting appropriately, such as shaking the tyre worker's hand when it was held out in a bid farewell; negotiating roads safely, including waiting until it was safe to cross; looking at and reading documents; and possessing sufficient manual dexterity to use his house keys to open the front door.

When the Defendant's expert reviewed the footage, he concluded the Claimant's condition was feigned. The Claimant's expert never commented on the footage but it was said by the Claimant's lawyers that the expert indicated he wanted nothing more to do with the case.

Arguments

At the s. 57 application hearing, the Claimant submitted that the Court could not justly determine the application without the litigation proceeding to a quantification of the claim. It was argued that only after hearing all the evidence and making appropriate factual findings would the Court then be in a position to determine whether the claim was 'fundamentally dishonesty' and whether it could be dismissed without 'substantial injustice' to the Claimant. In support of that submission, the Claimant relied on what the Supreme Court had said in *Summers v Fairclough Homes*, specifically dicta relating to the possibility of a strike out after trial where the Court had been able to "*make a proper assessment of both liability and quantum*".

Decision

HHJ Clarke rejected that submission for two principle reasons:

(a) First, s. 57(1)(a) provided that the Court could only find fundamental dishonesty once it had first found that the Claimant was entitled to damages on the claim, but it did not provide that the Court must first carry out a quantum assessment of the full claim before fundamental dishonesty could be found. She observed that the section could have said as much, if that was what was intended (at [35]).

(b) Secondly, she observed that, in s. 57(4), Parliament had imposed an obligation on the court to "*record the amount of damages that the court would have awarded to the claimant in respect of the primary claim but for dismissal of the claim*" [what

> the learned Judge referred to as the "honest part" of the claim] but that such an obligation only arose "*after: the court has found fundamental dishonesty; it has determined that dismissal of the claim would not cause substantial injustice to the Claimant; and it has decided to dismiss the claim. The reasons for this can be seen, I suggest, in ss 57(5), 57(6) and s57(7): so that credit is given for the lost 'honest part' of the claim when a claimant is ordered to pay the defendant's costs (s57(5)); and so that any court sentencing a claimant for a contempt arising out of the fundamental dishonesty, or in any related criminal proceedings, can take into account the lost damages for the 'honest part' of the claim and so avoid punishing him twice for the same behaviour (s57(6) and s57(7)). For neither reason, in my judgment, is a quantification of the full claim, including the 'fundamentally dishonest part' of it, necessary*" (at [37]).

HHJ Clarke held, at [37] that (emphasis added):

> "*For those reasons* ***I am satisfied that as a matter of law, a s57 application may be determined at any time after the claimant's entitlement to damages is established. Whether, in any case, it should be determined before a quantum trial will depend on whether it can be determined justly at that time. This will depend on all the circumstances of that particular case.*** *I can see the force in the Claimant's submission that by considering a s57 application after the liability trial but before full quantification of the claim the court is effectively embarking on a summary process. For that reason* ***I consider it is necessary for a court considering a s57 application in these circumstances to think carefully whether there are real grounds for believing that a fuller investigation will add to or alter the evidence relevant to the issues that it must determine, per Asplin J at [73] of Tesco Stores Ltd v Mastercard Inc. [2015] EWHC 1145.***"

Ultimately, HHJ Clarke found that the Claimant was presumed to have capacity to litigate; the diagnosis of a severe conversion disorder was not tenable - the Claimant's disability was feigned and there was no medical condition to account for it; it had been open to the Claimant to give evidence to answer the s. 57 application but he had not done so; the Claimant presented an "*egregiously untrue picture of [his] disabilities to the experts in this case*"; that he had been fundamentally dishonest in respect of his claim; and that the entirety of the claim should be dismissed, the Court being satisfied that no substantial injustice would be caused in so doing.

Paul Johnson v (1) Joseph Qainoo; (2) CIS General Insurance [2017] 6 WLUK 614 (Croydon County Court, 29/6/2017, DJ Bishop)

It may also be possible for the Defendant to make a successful 'early' s. 57 application, at an interim stage. That is what happened in the case of *Johnson.*

Facts

On the 1st September 2012 the Claimant was riding his bicycle when the First Defendant opened his car door, knocking the Claimant to the floor and causing him to sustain facial injuries. The Claimant brought a claim for personal injury and consequential losses, including a claim for loss of earnings pleaded in the sum of £85,000. The total claim was approximately £97,000. Breach of duty was admitted by the Defendant, as was causation of *some* injury.

In his Particulars of Claim the Claimant alleged that his work as a computer programmer and designer was adversely affected by reason of his injuries. He attached to his Particulars a Schedule of Loss in which he claimed he was a computer engineer and software developer, at the time he was subcontracted to a company called 'Viterable Software Invocation', and that, on behalf of that organisation, he had signed a contract to design, develop, build and install a networking platform for a third party company. The contract was said to be for eight weeks' work and worth £85,000 to the Claimant. By reason of his accident he said he was unable to fulfil that contract and so the company arranged for someone else to complete the work and the Claimant was paid nothing.

In its Defence, the Defendant alleged that the contract disclosed in support of the £85,000 loss of earning claim was a fabrication, having been crudely adapted from a contract between two Chinese companies that the Second Defendant's solicitor had found on the internet. The Claimant later provided a copy of another contract dated the 1st September 2012 (the day of the accident) which the Claimant allegedly signed in the morning before he was knocked off his bike. The Defendant asserted that this second contract was also a fabrication, not least because it was signed two years before the company with which the Claimant was purporting to contract had even been incorporated.

The Court gave Directions, requiring the Claimant to provide certain disclosure including proof of his professional qualifications, tax returns, and documentation evidencing the formation and registration of 'Viterable Software Invocation'. The Claimant provided no such documentation and, at trial, was ultimately shown not to possess the various qualifications he alleged.

The Defendant made an interim application for dismissal of the entirety of the claim pursuant to s. 57(2) on the basis that the Claimant had been 'fundamentally dishonest'.

The matter came before DJ Bishop. At the hearing of the application, the claim for £85,000 loss of earnings was formally abandoned. That did not, in DJ Bishop's view, "*relieve the claimant from the potential consequences of Section 57*"[1] (at [5]). The Claimant gave evidence and was cross-examined. The Judge was satisfied that the Claimant had fabricated both contracts on which he purported to rely; she concluded he

1 Such an approach being in accordance with the later decision of Jay J in *Roberts* (at [54]).

had lied to the Court on oath and in his written evidence; she considered that his claim for loss of earnings was fabricated purely for the purpose of obtaining money by deception. The Judge considered he had committed perjury and that she was "*utterly convinced that he has without doubt been fundamentally dishonest*". The claim was dismissed in its entirety, with the Judge assessing damages for the 'genuine' element of the claim.

Comment

The only immutable requirement prior to the making of an application under s. 57 is that the Claimant is entitled to damages in respect of the claim. It does not matter whether that entitlement arises as a result of a Court's determination of the issue of liability, or because the Defendant makes an admission.

As *Patel* makes clear, where the liability issue has been resolved it is not an absolute requirement that the Court must have also assessed the quantum of damages before considering, and determining, a s. 57 application [the decision in *Johnson*, in determining an *interim* s. 57 application, is also supportive of this approach]. That conclusion is unsurprising considering the wording of s. 57 itself, as HHJ Clarke observed. It is also unsurprising considering the duty imposed on the Court to further the Overriding Objective - it is suggested that there would be considerable force in a submission that determination of a s. 57 application at such a juncture has the potential benefit of avoiding a trial on quantum, which may be very costly and time consuming in terms of Court resources.

The general proposition that the Court *may* consider a s. 57 application at any time after the determination of the liability issue is subject to an important caveat that the Court should do so only where, in all the circumstances of the case, it is just to do so, and where a fuller investigation is unlikely to add to, or alter, the evidence which is germane to the issues before the Court. In many cases, perhaps in all but the clearest of cases where with strong *prima facie* evidence of dishonesty, it is suggested that the Court is likely to consider itself best served in determining the application after the conclusion of a trial on quantum.

In the overwhelming majority of cases proceeding on the small claims track and Fast Tracks, the approach taken in *Patel* is unlikely to be available for the simple reason that split trials are rare. In lower value, less complicated, and/or shorter Multi-Track trials, split trials are also highly uncommon. Where the case is listed for a trial on liability **and** quantum, and the Court is expecting to deal with all issues in the allotted time available, whilst it technically could do so if the evidence was clear, it is suggested that it is unlikely the Court would entertain an application under s. 57 part way through proceedings.

In the vast majority of cases, therefore, s. 57 applications are likely to be made orally by Counsel at the conclusion of the full trial. It is suggested that this is also likely to be the most sensible stage at which to make the application, and the stage at which such an application has the best prospects of success: the Judge will have heard all the evidence; the Defendant will have (presumably) made significant headway with the Claimant in cross-examination; the Judge will have had an opportunity to assess the Claimant and his/her credibility whilst giving evidence; and the Court is likely to consider that the Claimant has been given an adequate opportunity to explain any inconsistences/issues in his/her evidence.

In a liability admitted case it is technically possible to issue an 'early' application for determination of the s. 57 issue. A successful early interim application has the attractive benefit of saving costs, as well as bring the proceedings to a speedier resolution. An unsuccessful early application may also narrow the issues and/or promote settlement, which also has its own benefits. However, there are a number of significant potential drawbacks in making an early application, including:

(a) If the Defendant runs all the available arguments vis-à-vis 'fundamental dishonesty' at an interim stage, and loses, subject to further evidence coming to light during the course of the litigation there is essentially no basis for a Judge to make such a finding at the conclusion of the trial. In fact, absent any new evidence and/or change of circumstances, it is highly likely that the Defendant would be precluded from running the argument again at trial given it has already been considered and determined in the Claimant's favour;

(b) In pursuing the application at an early stage, the Defendant will have deployed its strongest arguments, thereby forewarning the Claimant as to the challenges which are likely to be made to his evidence at trial and enabling him/her to prepare accordingly;

(c) If the application is lost, it will increase the Defendant's costs exposure. It would not be surprising if any costs award made in the Claimant's favour at the conclusion of the application was assessed on the indemnity basis.

In the circumstances, it is suggested that only in the clearest of cases, where the evidence of dishonesty is compelling, should such an early, interim application be made. Although, naturally, the threat of such an application may be a powerful tool in the ongoing *inter partes* correspondence and may give a Claimant serious pause for thought as to whether to continue with the claim, discontinue, or accept a low settlement offer.

CHAPTER TWENTY TWO
THE ABSENCE OF A QUANTIFIED SCHEDULE OF LOSS

After dismissal of the entire claim, s. 57(4) of the 2015 Act requires the Court to assess the quantum of the 'genuine' element(s) of the claim in relation to which the Claimant would otherwise have been entitled to damages, so that it can carry out the off-setting exercise detailed in s. 57(5). However, what approach should the Court adopt where there is no finalised Schedule of Loss? In such circumstances, is the Court precluded from dismissal of the claim pursuant to s. 57(2) by reason of its' inability to carry out the s. 57(4) exercise? Or, perhaps, is the Court required to assess damages at nil, or in a way disadvantageous to the Claimant?

HHJ Clarke had to tackle some of these issues in *Patel v Arriva.* In *Patel,* the Schedule of Loss was unparticularised, leading the learned Judge to observe (at [4]):

> *"An amended particulars of claim and amended provisional schedule of loss were filed on 4 May 2016 and 5 May 2016 respectively. The Claimant's litigation friend, his son Chirag Patel, signed both documents with a statement of truth. The amended provisional schedule of loss runs to 8 pages of headline categorisation of past and future loss, but is entirely unparticularised as to narrative, as to relevant dates, and as to quantum. Each heading merely contains beside it "TBC"".*

The Judge then considered the competing arguments as to how she should approach the issue:

> *"100. Mr Jeffreys for the Defendants submits that all I am able to award is general damages for pain, suffering and loss of amenity res-*

> *ulting from the cardiac arrest, subarachnoid haemorrhage and anoxic brain injury, as the Claimant has not particularised the amended provisional schedule of loss. He submits that the appropriate category to consider in the Judicial College Guidelines is 3A(e) for a Minor Brain or Head Injury, with an uplifted range from £1940 to £11,200. I agree this is the correct category. The narrative is as follows: "In these cases brain damage, if any, will have been minimal. The level of the award will be affected by the following considerations: a) the severity of the initial injury b) the period taken to recover from any symptoms c) the extent of continuing symptoms d) the presence or absence of headaches The bottom of the bracket will reflect full recovery within a few weeks."*
>
> *101. Mr Hunjan for the Claimant submits that the Court cannot determine the s57 application at all, as it cannot carry out the quantification of damages required by s57(4) because the amended schedule of loss is unparticularised. He asks me to dismiss it for that reason.*

HHJ Clarke determined the issue in the Defendant's favour. She held as follows (emphasis added):

> *102. In my judgment it sits ill for the Claimant seek to shield himself from a dismissal of a claim where fundamental dishonesty has been found simply by his own failure to produce any meaningful schedule of loss during the many years that these proceedings have been afoot. Mr Hunjan concedes that the Claimant "could have had a stab" at particularising already incurred losses, but he submits that no direction has been made for an updated schedule of damages, and the Claimant cannot further particularise the claim without assistance from the whole gamut of experts listed above.*
>
> *[...]*

> *104. In relation to quantification of the claim, the court would have a much greater idea of the scope of the 'honest part' of the claim had the Claimant filed a schedule of loss which "draws together the scope of the claim", as Yip J puts it* [in the case of *Wright*], *rather than a blank schedule of headings.* ***I consider that the Claimant has had ample time since the s57 application was made in March 2018 to file even a partly particularised provisional schedule to cover the 'honest part' of the claim. The Claimant knew that this application might result in the court quantifying damages for the 'honest part' of the claim. If he has not done so, then I agree with the Defendants' submission that the court cannot assess anything other than general damages for pain suffering and loss of amenity. I cannot speculate on what the other losses may be."***

Comment

For understandable reasons, the Court was unimpressed at the suggestion that the Claimant's failure to produce a particularised Schedule of Loss led axiomatically to the conclusion that the Court could not therefore consider the application, nor dismiss the claim pursuant to s. 57(2). The Claimant's conduct was, rightly, criticised; he could not rely on his own failings to avoid the consequences of his dishonesty. In the absence of a Schedule, the Court had to do the best it could meaning simply assessing general damages for pain, suffering and loss of amenity, and declining to speculate on any other losses.

However, in *Patel*, the Court considered that the Claimant had had sufficient time to produce a Schedule, even if only provisional in nature. In circumstances where the Court is persuaded that the Claimant has *not* had sufficient time and/or the Court is otherwise not critical of the Claimant's conduct in not having provided a Schedule of Loss, what then? The position is not entirely clear. Arguably the Court could still try to do 'the best it can, on the evidence available', but that may seem to be somewhat unjust on the Claimant.

It is tentatively suggested that absence of a Schedule of Loss is likely to be of more relevance when the Court is considering whether it *should hear* an application under s. 57 at all (for example, at an interim stage, or following a trial on liability but before the quantum trial), and of less relevance in a situation where the Court has already decided to hear, and *is in the process of determining* such an application. A lack of criticism of the Claimant and/or his/her conduct, might reasonably lead the Court to decline to hear the application at an earlier/interim stage, given it cannot carry out the exercise in s. 57(4) and (5) and instead, to give directions for the progression of the claim to a hearing where the Claimant's case is properly set out in a Schedule and at which the allegations of dishonesty can be properly and fully determined. Such an approach would seem to accord with the comments of HHJ Clarke (at [37][1]).

1 Set out in Chapter 19 above.

SECTION (VI)

CONCLUSION

CHAPTER TWENTY THREE CONCLUDING REMARKS

Dishonest Claimants in personal injury claims are not a novel phenomenon; nor is the insurance industry's understandable desire to identify and expose dishonest claims. The implementation of QOCS has, however, undoubtedly resulted in a heightened level of scrutiny of claims by Defendants, and an increase in the frequency with which it is suggested, whether earlier in the litigation or at trial, that dishonesty is present. The reason for that is clear and obvious – Defendants wish to bring themselves within the scope of an exception to the QOCS regime in order to recover their otherwise irrecoverable costs. Whilst it might be argued that the very manner in which the system operates militates towards Defendants adopting such an approach, it might also perhaps be said that in some instances, it is employed somewhat hopefully in claims where, realistically, there is no discernible element of dishonesty.

Notwithstanding the QOCS provisions have now been in operation for a reasonable period of time, anecdotal evidence suggests there is still, regrettably, a wide-ranging disparity of approach and outcome as between individual District and Circuit Judges, as well as across different parts of the country, with some Judges seemingly highly receptive to submissions that the case is dishonest, and others notably less so. It is suggested the more recently decided authorities evidence a willingness by the High Court to find dishonesty allegations proven. It is to be hoped that this apparent divergence of approach continues to diminish, not least so that practitioners on both sides of the litigation can provide reasonably reliable advice to their clients.

The implementation of s. 57 of the 2015 Act represented a significant change to the existing law as it stood post *Summers v Fairclough Homes,* driven by policy considerations that a claimant who brings a dishonest claim should lose the entirety of that claim. In interpreting the provision, the Courts have understandably drawn on the earlier jurisprudence arising from the QOCS decisions and, in essence, through the judgments in *LOCOG* and *Pinkus* have affected a welcome harmonisation between the two.

There continue to be a reasonable number of appeals brought seeking to overturn lower courts refusals to make a finding of fundamental dishonesty; that appears unlikely to change in the near future.

The limits of the QOCS provisions and the ambit of s. 57 of the 2015 Act will continue to be explored in the higher courts in the coming years. The most fertile ground, at present, would appear to be the meaning and scope of the exception contained in s. 57(2) relating to 'substantial injustice' which no doubt will be the focus of more authoritative guidance in the near future.

MORE BOOKS BY LAW BRIEF PUBLISHING

A selection of our other titles available now:-

'Covid-19, Homeworking and the Law – The Essential Guide to Employment and GDPR Issues' by Forbes Solicitors
'Covid-19, Force Majeure and Frustration of Contracts – The Essential Guide' by Keith Markham
'Covid-19 and Criminal Law – The Essential Guide' by Ramya Nagesh
'Covid-19 and Family Law in England and Wales – The Essential Guide' by Safda Mahmood
'Covid-19 and the Implications for Planning Law – The Essential Guide' by Bob Mc Geady & Meyric Lewis
'Covid-19, Residential Property, Equity Release and Enfranchisement – The Essential Guide' by Paul Sams and Louise Uphill
'Covid-19, Brexit and the Law of Commercial Leases – The Essential Guide' by Mark Shelton
'Covid-19 and the Law Relating to Food in the UK and Republic of Ireland – The Essential Guide' by Ian Thomas
'A Practical Guide to the General Data Protection Regulation (GDPR) – 2nd Edition' by Keith Markham
'Ellis on Credit Hire – Sixth Edition' by Aidan Ellis & Tim Kevan
'A Practical Guide to Working with Litigants in Person and McKenzie Friends in Family Cases' by Stuart Barlow
'Protecting Unregistered Brands: A Practical Guide to the Law of Passing Off' by Lorna Brazell
'A Practical Guide to Secondary Liability and Joint Enterprise Post-Jogee' by Joanne Cecil & James Mehigan

'A Practical Guide to the Pre-Action RTA Claims Protocol for Personal Injury Lawyers' by Antonia Ford
'A Practical Guide to Neighbour Disputes and the Law' by Alexander Walsh
'A Practical Guide to Forfeiture of Leases' by Mark Shelton
'A Practical Guide to Coercive Control for Legal Practitioners and Victims' by Rachel Horman
'A Practical Guide to Rights Over Airspace and Subsoil' by Daniel Gatty
'Tackling Disclosure in the Criminal Courts – A Practitioner's Guide' by Narita Bahra QC & Don Ramble
'A Practical Guide to the Law of Driverless Cars – Second Edition' by Alex Glassbrook, Emma Northey & Scarlett Milligan
'A Practical Guide to TOLATA Claims' by Greg Williams
'Artificial Intelligence – The Practical Legal Issues' by John Buyers
'A Practical Guide to the Law of Prescription in Scotland' by Andrew Foyle
'A Practical Guide to the Construction and Rectification of Wills and Trust Instruments' by Edward Hewitt
'A Practical Guide to the Law of Bullying and Harassment in the Workplace' by Philip Hyland
'How to Be a Freelance Solicitor: A Practical Guide to the SRA-Regulated Freelance Solicitor Model' by Paul Bennett
'A Practical Guide to Prison Injury Claims' by Malcolm Johnson
'A Practical Guide to the Small Claims Track' by Dominic Bright
'A Practical Guide to Advising Clients at the Police Station' by Colin Stephen McKeown-Beaumont
'A Practical Guide to Antisocial Behaviour Injunctions' by Iain Wightwick
'Practical Mediation: A Guide for Mediators, Advocates, Advisers, Lawyers, and Students in Civil, Commercial, Business, Property, Workplace, and Employment Cases' by Jonathan Dingle with John Sephton
'The Mini-Pupillage Workbook' by David Boyle

'A Practical Guide to Crofting Law' by Brian Inkster
'A Practical Guide to Spousal Maintenance' by Liz Cowell
'A Practical Guide to the Law of Domain Names and Cybersquatting' by Andrew Clemson
'A Practical Guide to the Law of Gender Pay Gap Reporting' by Harini Iyengar
'A Practical Guide to the Rights of Grandparents in Children Proceedings' by Stuart Barlow
'NHS Whistleblowing and the Law' by Joseph England
'Employment Law and the Gig Economy' by Nigel Mackay & Annie Powell
'A Practical Guide to Noise Induced Hearing Loss (NIHL) Claims' by Andrew Mckie, Ian Skeate, Gareth McAloon
'An Introduction to Beauty Negligence Claims – A Practical Guide for the Personal Injury Practitioner' by Greg Almond
'Intercompany Agreements for Transfer Pricing Compliance' by Paul Sutton
'Zen and the Art of Mediation' by Martin Plowman
'A Practical Guide to the SRA Principles, Individual and Law Firm Codes of Conduct 2019 – What Every Law Firm Needs to Know' by Paul Bennett
'A Practical Guide to Adoption for Family Lawyers' by Graham Pegg
'A Practical Guide to Industrial Disease Claims' by Andrew Mckie & Ian Skeate
'A Practical Guide to Redundancy' by Philip Hyland
'A Practical Guide to Vicarious Liability' by Mariel Irvine
'A Practical Guide to Applications for Landlord's Consent and Variation of Leases' by Mark Shelton
'A Practical Guide to Relief from Sanctions Post-Mitchell and Denton' by Peter Causton
'A Practical Guide to Equity Release for Advisors' by Paul Sams
'A Practical Guide to Unlawful Eviction and Harassment' by Stephanie Lovegrove
'A Practical Guide to the Law Relating to Food' by Ian Thomas

'A Practical Guide to Financial Services Claims' by Chris Hegarty
'The Law of Houses in Multiple Occupation: A Practical Guide to HMO Proceedings' by Julian Hunt
'A Practical Guide to Unlawful Eviction and Harassment' by Stephanie Lovegrove
'A Practical Guide to Solicitor and Client Costs' by Robin Dunne
'Occupiers, Highways and Defective Premises Claims: A Practical Guide Post-Jackson – 2nd Edition' by Andrew Mckie
'A Practical Guide to Financial Ombudsman Service Claims' by Adam Temple & Robert Scrivenor
'A Practical Guide to Advising Schools on Employment Law' by Jonathan Holden
'A Practical Guide to Running Housing Disrepair and Cavity Wall Claims: 2nd Edition' by Andrew Mckie & Ian Skeate
'A Practical Guide to Holiday Sickness Claims – 2nd Edition' by Andrew Mckie & Ian Skeate
'Arguments and Tactics for Personal Injury and Clinical Negligence Claims' by Dorian Williams
'A Practical Guide to QOCS and Fundamental Dishonesty' by James Bentley
'A Practical Guide to Drone Law' by Rufus Ballaster, Andrew Firman, Eleanor Clot
'A Practical Guide to Compliance for Personal Injury Firms Working With Claims Management Companies' by Paul Bennett
'A Practical Guide to the Landlord and Tenant Act 1954: Commercial Tenancies' by Richard Hayes & David Sawtell
'A Practical Guide to Dog Law for Owners and Others' by Andrea Pitt
'RTA Allegations of Fraud in a Post-Jackson Era: The Handbook – 2nd Edition' by Andrew Mckie
'RTA Personal Injury Claims: A Practical Guide Post-Jackson' by Andrew Mckie
'On Experts: CPR35 for Lawyers and Experts' by David Boyle
'An Introduction to Personal Injury Law' by David Boyle

'A Practical Guide to Chronic Pain Claims' by Pankaj Madan
'A Practical Guide to Claims Arising from Fatal Accidents' by James Patience
'A Practical Guide to Subtle Brain Injury Claims' by Pankaj Madan

www.ingramcontent.com/pod-product-compliance
Lightning Source LLC
LaVergne TN
LVHW022048200926
848481LV00003B/830